ADEQUATE DECISION RULES FOR PORTFOLIO CHOICE PROBLEMS

Adequate Decision Rules for Portfolio Choice Problems

THILO GOODALL

palgrave

First published 2002 by
PALGRAVE
Houndmills, Basingstoke, Hampshire RG21 6XS and
175 Fifth Avenue, New York, N.Y. 10010
Companies and representatives throughout the world

PALGRAVE is the new global academic imprint of St. Martin's Press LLC Scholarly and Reference Division and Palgrave Publishers Ltd (formerly Macmillan Press Ltd).

ISBN 0–333–99432–9 paperback

This book is printed on paper suitable for recycling and made from fully managed and sustained forest sources.

A catalogue record for this book is available from the British Library.

Library of Congress Cataloging-in-Publication Data

Goodall, Thilo, 1965–
Adequate decision rules for portfolio choice problems / Thilo Goodall.
p. cm. — (Finance and capital markets series)
Originally presented as the author's thesis—University of Freiburg im Breisgau, 2000.
Includes bibliographical references and index.
ISBN 0–333–99432–9 (cloth)
1. Portfolio management—Mathematical models. I. Title. II. Series.

HG4529.5 .G67 2002
332.6'01'51—dc21 2002020830

Editing and origination by
Aardvark Editorial, Mendham, Suffolk

10 9 8 7 6 5 4 3 2 1
11 10 09 08 07 06 05 04 03 02

Printed in Great Britain by
Antony Rowe Limited, Chippenham and Eastbourne

for

Monika Minder

Contents

List of Figures

Preface

The existing literature on portfolio choice theory and its related fields is nothing short of overwhelming. The immediate reaction of anyone developing a deeper interest in the field is to try to categorise the different contributions. The challenge is to arrange layer after layer of analyses, amendments and enhancements around the seminal work of Markowitz, and the much forgotten contribution of Roy, finding for each and every one a proper place and displaying its links to all others.

As in a mind-map, links spread out in all different directions. Normative or positive stances are adopted, modelling or description is pursued, and experiments or observations are employed, or simply intuition and introspection. Soon, the mind-map becomes enormous, covering areas ranging from history to psychology and mathematics. In the end, the map turns into something resembling a fractal object rather than displaying the hoped for linear structure.

Fortunately, being reminiscent of a fractal object, some patterns of the map repeat themselves. Self-similarities, or common themes, can be found. One is the frequent reappearance of a specific definition of rationality. Another is the frequent reappearance of expected values.

Thus, when taking a step back, a research interest arises that differs from adding detail. Viewing the entire field of portfolio choice from a higher perspective reveals patterns that warrant analysis. What has caused themes and ingredients to become widespread and common?

Why and when have they been introduced? Is the reasoning sound, or can it be contested, and if so, what alternatives can be proposed? These questions are addressed here. Aspects common to the entire field are illuminated, leading to questioning assumptions that have passed unquestioned for quite some time. Aiding in the task are fundamental building blocks of decision theory and econometric theory.

There has been other aid as well. It is common practice, and good practice, to put down in writing one's gratitude for all the contributions by every contributor. Since the importance of any contribution and the gratitude felt for it are difficult to measure, contrary to common practice, acknowledgements are listed in order of appearance.

First to appear was Dr Klaus Kammerer, who introduced me to methodology and decision theory, and whom I have to thank for his incessant interest in discussing every aspect of the work, always resulting in new thoughts and ideas. I owe gratitude to Professor Dr Dietrich Lüdeke, who has accompanied my work from beginning to end, and whose insights and stimulating comments have taken it further than I had originally hoped. I also owe gratitude to Dr Peter Saacke and Dr Andreas Schmidt-von Rhein for their valuable comments and suggestions that helped me focus on what is original and important.

I am also much indebted to Frau Elsbeth Bernoulli-Eidenbenz for granting me privileged access to the family chronicles of the Bernoulli family. The works of members of this celebrated family have shaped decision theory and portfolio choice to the present day. Nothing could have motivated me more than learning from first hand accounts of the work, life and characters of Jacob, Nicholas and Daniel Bernoulli.

Well, almost nothing. Constantly encouraging me and raising my spirits was she to whom this book is dedicated. Certainly hers was the most valuable contribution, though it is impossible to adequately express my appreciation here.

THILO GOODALL

List of Abbreviations

Capital letters set in boldface:

A	set of actions
G	set of gambles
N	set of states of nature
R	set of results
U	set of utilities

Greek letters:

Σ	matrix of variances and covariances of the assets' returns
$\Phi(.)$	$= \varphi(u(R))$, random variable that is a function of a gamble's results
$\Psi(.)$	decision rule, that is, preference index defined over the set **G** of all gambles
α	fixed probability
δ	threshold of utility
$\varphi(.)$	risk attitude function
μ	expected value
π	general preference index
ρ	correlation coefficient
σ	standard deviation

$\omega(.)$	$= \varphi(u(r))$, combined function of utility evaluation and risk attitude
ξ	percentile
$\psi(.)$	risk preference function

Latin letters:

A	minimum variance portfolio
B	maximum expected value portfolio
C	most preferred portfolio, optimal overall portfolio
$Cov[.]$	covariance
CP rule	'cumulative probability' rule
$E[.]$	expected value
EU	expected utility
$F(.)$	cumulative distribution function
G	gamble, or portfolio
LPM	lower partial moment
MFE	mean forecast error
MSFE	mean squared forecast error
OR	optimal risky portfolio
$P(.)$	probability
R_i	random variable, which values are the results of a gamble
SV	semi-variance
T	time index denoting the investment horizon
U_i	random variable, which values are the utilities associated with the results of a gamble
$V[.]$	variance
W	random variable, which values are the investor's wealth, or the value of a portfolio
d	threshold of return
i	$= 1...n$, index of actions
j	$= 1...m$, index of states of nature
h	index of assets in a portfolio
$\mathbf{s}$	summer vector, that is, a column vector containing the value 1 in every row
t	$= 1...\tau$, time index denoting investment periods
$u(.)$	utility function
w	wealth, value of a portfolio
$\mathbf{x}$	vector of the weights of all assets in a portfolio

CHAPTER 1

Introduction

Hidden beneath its many facets and different aspects, veiled by inexhaustibly many contributions on all those different aspects, and obscured by a swarm of buzz words originating from the trading floors and back offices of the investment community, lies the plain core problem of portfolio choice theory: how to choose. Portfolio choice, or portfolio selection, is concerned with how much of a given wealth to devote to individual assets, that is, which weights to assign to each asset, that is, which portfolio to choose. Portfolio choice theory is thus nothing but an application of decision theory. It should be treated within this framework, unperturbed by all the buzzing.

In decision theory, it has proven convenient to rely on decision rules whenever possible. They identify the single most preferred action among a set of possible actions. Since portfolio choice problems are a mere application of decision theory, decision rules have entered portfolio choice theory as well. Here they identify the single most preferred portfolio among a set of all possible portfolios. Decision rules have become a tool widespread in decision theory and all its applications. The first purpose of this treatise is to analyse the decision rules that have been proposed for portfolio choice problems. The second purpose is to recommend some alternatives.

When analysing the decision rules that are prominent in portfolio selection theory today, it becomes strikingly apparent that two related contributions have to this day an overwhelming influence. The first is Daniel Bernoulli's solution for the so-called 'St Petersburg paradox', which he proposed in 1738. The second is the von Neumann and Morgenstern 'expected utility principle', which they designed in 1944 under the inspiration of an article written by Menger in 1934 on the St Petersburg paradox.

Daniel Bernoulli applies a 'moral expectation'[1] to the possible gains of the St Petersburg game. He thus proposes to equate the 'fair' entrance fee to the game with the expected value of its evaluated gains, rather than with the expected value of its nominal gains. His proposal helped to entrench the expected value's position in early decision theory. In its wake expected values have become the main component of the vast majority of decision rules.

The influence of the work of von Neumann and Morgenstern has been twofold. First, their expected utility principle increased decision theory's reliance on expected values. But their influence went further. They dubbed their decision principle 'rational', a claim that was reinforced by an axiomatic embedding. Many authors considered the axioms so fundamental that a compulsion evolved to base all normative decision theory, as well as a good part of descriptive decision theory, on them. Only decision rules that complied with the axioms, and thus with the expected utility principle, were seen fit to be labelled 'rational' and considered serious contributions to normative or descriptive decision theory. Not surprisingly, decision rules proposed for portfolio selection problems were also required to meet this standard definition of 'rationality'.

It will be argued here that no definition of 'rationality' is indisputable, no matter whether it is based on a set of axioms or not. In the end, nothing but mere opinion can be brought forward to justify any view on rationality. The arguments given in the following chapters will thus clear the way of any obstacles erected by the traditional definition of 'rationality'. The discussion can then focus on the predominance of expected values and the question of in which kind of decision situations can their use be supported.

As it will turn out, expected values have found explicit or implicit support in the law of large numbers. But the law of large numbers can only be applied to decision situations that are characterised by infinitely many repeats, and in which the individual is concerned only about the simple average of all results.[2] Such situations may occur in the traditional application of decision theory, games of chance, but they almost never occur in the field of portfolio choice. Here, situations of no or only finitely many repeats are much more common, and other results than the simple average of all outcomes can have importance. The law of large numbers cannot support the use of expected values in such situations. It must thus be deemed inadequate to recommend expected values for such situations under implicit or explicit reference to the law of large numbers.

The analysis will lead to recommending some alternative decision rules. Their application will be discussed and graphically illustrated. To support these decision rules, they will be labelled 'adequate' for specific decision situations. Apparently, a definition of 'adequacy' is needed. In and by itself, 'adequacy' is an empty phrase, just like 'rationality' is.

In defining 'adequacy', it will prove helpful to analyse portfolio choice problems within a proper framework. The framework here defined 'proper' is the field of decisions under Knightian risk. In decision situations under Knightian risk the main problem is not that a decision must be made. Decisions must also be made in decision situations under certainty. The main problem and characteristic of decision situations under Knightian risk is that the result of any decision is uncertain. The decision problem is thus related to the problem of forecasting the outcome of a chance experiment, and may be guided by evaluating the costs of false prediction. Looking at the problem of decisions under Knightian risk from this related, but in the context of portfolio choice theory never considered perspective, will lead to a definition of 'adequacy'.

To accomplish these aims, a short review of decision theory is needed. It is given in Chapter 2. The field of decision theory that may be applied to portfolio selection problems will be defined, and the stage will be set for all following analyses.

Great care will be taken to differentiate between normative and descriptive decision theory, in order to avoid any confusion of arguments applicable to one field but not the other. This distinction will aid in the analysis given in Chapter 3, which discusses some of the decision rules that are prominent today in portfolio selection theory. This discussion will illustrate the expected value's historic role and influence. Accordingly, the chapter's structure follows to a not insignificant extent the history of thought on decision theory.

But the discussion of Chapter 3 not only illustrates the historic influences. The analysis of the prominent decision rules' dependence on expected values lays the foundation for defining 'adequacy' in Chapter 4. The definition of adequacy will be based on the necessary congruence between the decision rule, the decision situation it is proposed for, and any implicit or explicit support for the proposal. This congruence will serve as the starting point for designing decision rules for such decision situations that can be deemed relevant in the field of portfolio selection.

To make all decision rules comparable and to facilitate their analysis, standardised notations and terms will be used. Confusion between different concepts is thus avoided, albeit at the price of using notations and terms that sometimes differ slightly from those commonly used and easily recognised. Otherwise, the decision rules will be described as originally designed.

Throughout the treatise, the close link between decision theory, portfolio choice, and mathematical statistics will be emphasised. Having recourse to mathematical statistics will illuminate how and when its theorems can aid in proposing a decision rule for situations of Knightian risk. To emphasise the close link, decision situations that can be described in terms of probability distributions will generally be referred to as 'gambling situations'. After all, 'the classical theory of probability was devoted mainly to a study of the gambler's gain, which is again a random variable; in fact, every random variable can be interpreted as the gain of a real or imaginary gambler in a suitable game'.[3] 'Gambling situations' are thus taken as the general setting. All of what follows could indeed be discussed and analysed in general terms, including the situations involving portfolio choice problems and the decision rules proposed for them. Nevertheless, when portfolio choice problems are referred to, the term 'gamble' will be replaced by the terms 'investment' or 'portfolio'.

Notes

1 According to Sheynin (1972) Daniel Bernoulli did not use the term 'moral expectation'. It was coined by G. Cramér in a letter to Nicholas Bernoulli (the letter is published in D. Bernoulli (1738), pp. 33–5). The term will nevertheless be used here for D. Bernoulli's solution.

2 The law of large numbers comes in several versions. See Feller (1968), pp. 243–63. The assumptions discussed in this treatise are common to all versions. No distinction between versions need thus be made, and the general term can and will be used.

3 Feller (1968), p. 212.

CHAPTER 2

Risk and Decision

2.1 DECISION THEORY AND PORTFOLIO CHOICE

Every investor faces a decision regarding which assets to choose for his or her portfolio. Portfolio choice theory is thus about making decisions, and an application of decision theory. It seems appropriate to treat portfolio choice problems as decisions that are to be made in an uncertain environment.

In such an environment, individuals are not absolutely sure of the result of any particular action. If uncertainty does not stem from the acts of a competitor or an adversary, the result of any action will simply depend on unknown future events. To discuss the ways in which individuals make or should make their decisions facing an unknown future, Knight (1921) uses the term 'risk' to refer to situations in which the individual feels able to attach 'degrees of belief' or 'probabilities' to all possible states of nature.[1] He uses the term 'uncertainty' to refer to situations in which the individual feels unable to attach any such 'probabilities'.[2] Portfolio choice problems may be defined to belong to the former category, that is, to situations of Knightian risk. Since any topic should be analysed within its relevant framework, a repetition of the basic notations and concepts of the theory of 'decision under risk' will prove helpful.

Situations of Knightian risk are defined by four different sets: the set of actions, the set of states of the world, the set of results, and the set of utilities. The set of utilities is necessary because all results need to be evaluated. The sets may be considered discrete or continuous. For presentational ease they shall for the moment be assumed to be discrete, as well as finite.

The set of actions comprises all 'actions', or 'strategies', among which the individual may choose in a given situation. Let $\mathbf{A} = \{a_1, a_2, ..., a_n\}$ denote this set of all n actions conceived possible. The result of a chosen action depends on which 'state of nature', or 'state of the world', will pertain in the future. The second set thus comprises all states of nature the individual conceives possible. Let $\mathbf{N} = \{n_1, n_2, ..., n_m\}$ denote this set of all m states, assumed to be disjunctive. To each pairing (a_i, n_j) the individual might then assign a value r_{ij} indicating the 'result', or 'consequence', or 'state of the person', or 'outcome', of the action taken under the state of nature pertaining. Let $\mathbf{R}$ denote this set of all $n \times m$ results, where each element $r_{ij} \in \mathbf{R}$ is determined by a_i and n_j.

Most authors prefer to describe such situations as if they were objective ones, but it must be remembered that the sets of all possible actions and of all possible states of nature are as seen by the individual.[3] That all possible actions and states of nature are known to, or being considered by, the individual is an additional and unnecessary assumption. It is the individual who shapes the decision problem through his or her perception of the situation.

The subjective character becomes even more apparent by recognising the necessity to have the individual evaluate the results. By themselves the results bear no meaning. To be able to choose in some way or other among the actions, the individual has to express his or her preferences among the results. He or she has to evaluate them, and be able to order them accordingly. Such evaluations are clearly subjective. Each individual will evaluate the possible results quite differently, depending on personal tastes and circumstances.

Under certain conditions regarding the coherence of the individual's preferences, which will be discussed in section 2.2, the preference relations may be stated in terms of a function, $u(.)$, that assigns a real-valued number to every result in $\mathbf{R}$.[4] This real-valued function will here be called a 'utility function'. Decisions are then governed by the set $\mathbf{U}$ of all conceived utilities. Unfortunately, the term 'utility' is often used ambiguously. It may thus be necessary to clearly state that utilities as described here provide for a preference ordering of results. Very often, the term 'utility' is used to refer to a preference ordering of actions. In many such cases, it is not always clearly stated that the results have to be evaluated before a decision can be made. The set of utilities attributed to the results is not always explicitly mentioned.[5]

To all possible states of nature let the individual attach a 'degree of belief' or 'probability' $P(n_j)$, or P_j for short.[6] These probabilities must again be regarded as subjective, adding to the subjective character of all decision problems. It can and has been argued that subjective probabilities are the only type of probability that can be put on a sound basis.[7] But the analysis will remain the same, no matter whether probabilities are considered objective or subjective, as long as they obey Kolmogorov's (1933) basic axioms of probability theory. To facilitate further analysis, the applicability of these axioms is assumed. Probabilities will be treated as non-negative, summable and normed to unity.

Having introduced probabilities, it comes as no surprise that the theory of mathematical statistics plays a major role in decisions under Knightian risk. The situation given above shall thus now be described using statistical quantities and terminology. The possible states of nature, n_j, can be interpreted as the outcomes of a chance experiment having sample space **N**. The outcome of this chance experiment determines the result of the action taken. These results are given by a bivariate function $r_{ij} = h(a_i, n_j)$. For each action this function defines a sample space $\mathbf{R}_i$, being a subspace of **R**. Since the utility of each result is measured in real-valued numbers $u_{ij} = u(h(a_i, n_j))$, the utilities associated with a particular action are given by a real-valued function defined over the sample space $\mathbf{R}_i$. The utilities can hence be regarded as the values taken on by a random variable denoted $U(a_i)$, or U_i for short.[8]

Given the probability distribution on the set **N** of all conceived states of nature, the choice of any particular action a_i will induce a probability distribution on the subset $\mathbf{U}_i$ of the corresponding utilities.[9] A choice among the actions a_i is thus tantamount to a choice among the random variables U_i. Each U_i is defined over its sample space $\mathbf{U}_i$, and has a distinct probability distribution. Decisions are hence choices among random variables and their distributions. The random variables may be referred to as 'gambles', or 'prospects', or 'lotteries'. Each gamble, denoted G_i, comprises of a set of utilities and a set of associated probabilities. Each pairing (u_{ij}, p_j) constitutes a 'chance' of the respective gamble.[10] Choices among the random variables U_i or their distributions are governed solely by the distributions' characteristics.

It now becomes apparent which assumptions are needed to treat portfolio choice as a special case of decisions under Knightian risk. Portfolios are built by investing fractions of the overall investable wealth in single assets. Portfolios differ only in the fractions that are assigned to the single assets. These fractions are commonly referred to as weights.[11] The return on any single asset after a given period will depend on a multitude of economic and non-economic factors. The bundled influence exerted by these factors is equivalent to the influence of the 'state of nature'. If the individual feels able to attribute probabilities to the 'states of nature', they may be regarded as the outcome of a chance experiment. This chance experiment determines the result, that is, the return on an investment in any single asset. Returns are thus real-valued variables defined over a sample space, and therefore random variables.[12]

Furthermore, any portfolio's return is equal to the weighted sum of the single assets' returns it comprises. Any portfolio's return is thus a function of the single assets' returns. The utility of a portfolio is also a function of the utility of the single assets' returns. Being functions of random variables, the portfolio's return and its assigned utility are thus random variables as well.[13] Each portfolio is associated with a distinct set of weights, and thus with a distinct random variable U_i having a distinct probability distribution. Actions are equivalent to choosing weights, and choosing weights is equivalent to choosing among the random variables U_i and their respective distributions. Thus, if it is assumed that the individual feels able to attach probabilities to all possible returns of any single asset, returns on investments can be regarded as random variables, and portfolio choice problems translate into problems of decision under Knightian risk.

2.2 DECISION RULES

Any decision situation may be analysed from two different perspectives, which distinguish two major disciplines of decision theory. The first discipline, descriptive decision theory, describes observed decision behaviour. It analyses which variables affect individual perception of decision situations and how choices are actually made. The second discipline, normative decision theory, provides recommendations as to how decisions should be made. To support these recommendations in some manner, they are typically declared 'plausible' or 'rational'. Defining 'rationality' thus plays an important role in normative decision theory.

Descriptive and normative decision theory thus have distinct objectives. Quite clearly, defining rational behaviour differs from describing observed, and possibly inconsistent, behaviour. But despite this fundamental difference, there exist common features. One such feature is the use of a common formalised setting, such as the one described in section 2.1. Another common feature is the use of decision rules, which provide a convenient tool in both fields. Decision rules are real-valued functions $\Psi(.)$ defined over the set **G** of all gambles. They assign a real-valued number to each gamble such that the most preferred one is attributed the highest number.[14] Decision rules thus define the preference ordering among the gambles by acting as a preference index.

They are in this respect very much like utility functions and may, of course, be called utility functions as well. But in this treatise, the terms 'utility function' and 'decision rule' will be used to refer to different kinds of evaluations. Utility functions will be defined over sets of possible results of a chance experiment. They will express individual evaluations of results. Decision rules, in contrast, will be defined over sets of gambles. They will express individual evaluations of entire gambles and their distributions. The difference between the two concepts is quite straightforward. Indeed, even if two individuals agreed on the utility of each and every result of a gamble, they might still value the gamble itself quite differently. One individual may emphasise highly probable results, another might look for highly valued ones, even if less probable.

Decision rules are thus preference indices, applied to the set **G** of all gambles among which the individual may choose in a given decision situation. Each gamble G_i is defined over a set $\mathbf{U}_i$, consisting of the utilities assigned to all possible results of G_i. Since assigned utilities are nothing more than preference indices themselves, the use of decision rules requires that preference indices be applicable to both **G** and **R**.

If applicable, preference indices provide a convenient way to indicate preference relations. Such preference relations may be defined as weak or strong relations. Defined over a set **E** of unspecified elements e_i, weak relations are commonly denoted $e_i \preceq e_j$, meaning that element e_i is not preferred to element e_j. Strong relations are commonly denoted $e_i \prec e_j$, indicating that e_j is strictly preferred to e_i.

Debreu (1954) shows under which general conditions preference indices may be used to state such preference relations, that is, under which general conditions there exists a continuous function $\pi(.)$ such that $e_i \prec e_j$ is equivalent to $\pi(e_i) < \pi(e_j)$. These conditions are commonly denoted the 'ordering axioms' and will, though well known, be repeated here. They cast some light on the limitations of both disciplines of decision theory. To enhance readability, they will be stated for strong preference relations.[15]

1. *Completeness*

   For any two elements e_i and e_j of the set **E**, it is necessary that one of the following statements can always be made:

	$e_i \prec e_j$	(e_j is preferred to e_i)
or	$e_i \succ e_j$	(e_i is preferred to e_j)
or	$e_i \sim e_j$	(e_i is indifferent to e_j)

2. *Reflexivity*

   For any two elements e_i and e_j of the set **E**

   $$e_i = e_j \Rightarrow e_i \sim e_j$$

   A definition of identity is needed as well.[16]

3. *Transitivity*

   For any three elements e_i, e_j and e_k of the set **E**

   $$e_i \prec e_j \wedge e_j \prec e_k \Rightarrow e_i \prec e_k$$

Under these conditions there exists a continuous function, which ranks the elements e_i along an ordinal scale, that is, a preference index. This function is defined up to any positive monotonic transformation. But ordinal scales are rarely used. In decision theory in general, and in portfolio choice theory in particular, almost all decision rules are based on differences in the utilities the results provide.[17] Thus, differences need to be evaluated, for which cardinal scales are needed. Given some additional axioms that provide for an evaluation of utility differences, the existence of a cardinal utility function may be proven, which is defined up to any positive linear transformation.[18] These additional axioms are of no specific importance here and shall not be stated.

The important result is that the above conditions, together with all additional ones not stated here, must be met by both the sets **U** and **G**. Only then does there exist a continuous function that ranks results according to the individual's preference relations among these results. This function will here be called a 'utility function'. And only then does there exist a continuous function that ranks gambles according to the individual's preference relations among these gambles. This latter function will be called here a 'decision rule'.

Any application of decision rules in either normative or descriptive decision theory is thus based on Kolmogorov's probability axioms and on Debreu's ordering axioms. Since this treatise is exclusively on decision rules, a general discussion on the nature of normative and descriptive decision rules is advisable, as well as a discussion on the applicability of Kolmogorov's and Debreu's axioms. Some of the arguments given in Chapters 3 and 4 will have recourse to the arguments made here.

With respect to normative decision rules, the following has to be observed. The goal of normative decision theory is to recommend how decisions should be made. Of course, any such recommendation is in its core just an expression of opinion. There cannot and there does not exist any objective justification or any common measure for evaluating such a recommendation.

Instead, proponents of normative decision rules try to find support for their recommendation by declaring them 'plausible' or 'rational'. Unfortunately, any definition of 'rationality' is also nothing more than an expression of opinion. All that a definition of 'rationality' can achieve is to aid in gaining general acceptance for the proposed decision rule. Widespread acceptance is the only backing a normative decision rule can get. Such widespread acceptance would be easily achievable if there was a conclusive definition of 'rationality'. For example, a definition of 'rationality' that was placed within a definition of 'logical' behaviour could expect to achieve widespread or even general acceptance. Such a definition is impossible. Suffice it to note that the violation of Debreu's axioms cannot be dismissed as 'illogical'. Intransitivities, for example, do not violate the laws of logic. The framework of logic can thus only serve as a necessary condition of such a definition.

It is impossible to arrive at a conclusive definition of 'rationality' that is universally valid. 'Rationality' has to be defined without any directive from other fields, and may be defined in many different ways.[19] Normative decision rules are thus both unjustifiable and irrefutable, but vulnerable to a redefinition of 'rational behaviour'.

The ordering axioms have also proven the open flank of descriptive decision theory. Proponents of descriptive decision theory will claim that empirical testing alone can validate or falsify their decision rules. Unfortunately, empirical evidence on the violation of the ordering axioms is readily available. Intransitivities were very soon found by May (1954). The empirical works of Allais (1986), Grether and Plott (1979), and of Kahneman and Tversky (1979), also cast doubt on the ordering axioms' empirical validity, although not designed to test them directly.

Strictly speaking, the observed violations of Debreu's axioms deny proponents of descriptive decision theory the use of decision rules altogether. To be able to use decision rules, proponents of descriptive decision theory must thus postulate or assume that the ordering axioms are obeyed. This unsatisfactory condition is avoided here. The decision rules discussed in Chapter 4 are declared normative.

In contrast, calling for subjective probabilities to follow Kolmogorov´s axioms seems to cause few problems for both normative and descriptive decision theory. As for their use in normative decision theory, there is no serious objection to regarding someone who ignores them as 'irrational'. Indeed, some justification for obeying them, especially for the postulated summability of probabilities, is provided by Ramsey (1931), de Finetti (1937) and Savage (1954). As for their use in descriptive decision theory, it may suffice to remark that probabilities have entered everyday life in such a way that it does not seem untenable to assume all individuals consider them, knowingly or unknowingly, as non-negative, summable, as well as normed to unity.

Another observation must be made. Despite their distinct objectives, normative decision theory and descriptive decision theory share many common features. The most prevalent one is the use of utilities and the subsequent dependence on Debreu's ordering axioms. Together with the common use of decision rules, this has led to an unfortunate and continuing blurring of the clear distinction between normative and descriptive decision theory. The clearest manifestation of this blurring is an exchange of totally unjustified criticism across the two fields. Often enough, normative decision rules are treated as if they were designed to describe observed behaviour. They are put to empirical testing to evaluate their descriptive power, and are redesigned according to empirical findings.[20] But the fundamental difference between the two disciplines is completely disregarded if normative theories are refuted as incongruent with observed behaviour. After all, normative theories cannot be falsified using empirical findings. They need not consider observed behaviour. Even if all individuals behaved in a similar fashion, their behaviour need not be recommendable, simply because it is common and widespread. Proponents of normative decision theory may thus argue that it is irrelevant how individuals actually make decisions. Empirical findings are of no value to them.

Proponents of descriptive decision theory may in turn argue that described behaviour need not be 'rational'. Descriptive theory need not consider recommended behaviour. They may even consider making recommendations on how to choose completely useless.

Each side is thus immune to hostilities from the other. Arguments for or against normative theories cannot be based on descriptive theories, and vice versa. Both theories have their legitimate objectives, and their perspectives must not be confused when the use of specific decision rules is approved or rejected. Decision rules cannot be discussed on grounds of alleged 'irrationality' or 'contradictions to observed behaviour' without considering their specific normative or descriptive character.

When discussing decision rules in Chapter 3, arguments that stem from the normative perspective will thus be separated from arguments that stem from the descriptive one. The focus of the discussion in Chapter 3 lies on the normative aspects, and normative decision rules are proposed in Chapter 4. Arguments stemming from the field of descriptive decision theory are only discussed if they have gained some prominence, or if they have led to alternative proposals.

Notes

1 There are other interpretations of Knight's work, see for example Hoskins (1973), but this seems the prevalent one.
2 The term 'uncertainty' is often used to refer both to situations of Knightian 'risk' and Knightian 'uncertainty'.
3 Stegmüller (1973).
4 Debreu (1954).
5 Example given in DeGroot (1982).
6 It is conceivable that the individual considers the states of nature pertaining in the future as dependent on his or her actions, in which case the probabilities will have to be attached directly to the utilities.
7 DeGroot (1982), p. 279.
8 Defining the state of nature or the result themselves as random variables would require their outcomes to be real-valued numbers.
9 The sets $\mathbf{R}_i$ and $\mathbf{U}_i$ need not be of the same order, given the possibility that $u_{ij} = u_{ij+k}$ for some $k \neq 0$.
10 If the set $\mathbf{N}$ is discrete, the associated sample spaces $\mathbf{U}_i = \{u_{i1}, u_{i2}, ..., u_{im}\}$ are also discrete. Every element and subset of $\mathbf{U}_i$ then defines an event. If the set $\mathbf{N}$ is continuous, probabilities are assigned to subsets of the sample spaces $\mathbf{U}_i$, elements of which define events.
11 A single asset may be considered a portfolio with all weights but one equal to zero. In the following the term 'portfolio' may thus also denote just one asset.
12 In contrast to this special application, the results in a general decision problem are not necessarily real-valued numbers and therefore cannot always be defined as random variables.
13 It is convenient to assume that the utility of a portfolio is equal to the weighted sum of all assets' utilities. All that is needed for this assumption are additive utilities. However, the specific form of the function is irrelevant at this stage. Any function of one or more random variables is a random variable itself.
14 It is redundant to state explicitly that a decision rule includes the instruction to 'choose the action with the highest preference index'.

15 There are different ways to state the ordering axioms. The following is taken from Krelle (1968), pp. 6–12 and 123–6. In addition, two more axioms of rather topological nature are needed; see Debreu (1959), p. 56.

16 In case of e_i and e_j being elements of the set **G** of all gambles, they are defined as identical if their corresponding distributions are identical.

17 The simple maximin and maximax rules are exceptions.

18 Schneeweiß (1963).

19 Krelle (1968), pp. 138–67.

20 See, for example, Buschena and Zilberman (1994a).

CHAPTER 3

Analysis of Prominent Decision Rules

3.1 CHARACTERISATION OF DECISION RULES PROMINENT IN PORTFOLIO CHOICE

Portfolio choice problems have been shown to be special cases of decisions under Knightian risk. Investments are gambles, because the investments' results, and the utility they provide, depend on the outcome of a chance experiment. If portfolio selection is a special case of decision theory, and if Debreu's axioms are taken as valid, portfolio selection problems may be solved by applying decision rules. The decision rules that have, or have had, some importance in portfolio choice theory will now be characterised. They will be analysed in the following chapters.

Decision rules differ with respect to how much they utilise the information provided by the gambles' distributions. The kind of information used reveals something about the proposed or assumed evaluation of a decision situation. Decision rules may be characterised accordingly. They then fall into two major approaches.[1]

The first, called the 'classical approach', uses decision rules which are functions of the distribution's parameters.[2] Rather than utilising all information provided by the entire distribution of a gamble, classical decision rules utilise only some distribution parameters, like the mean, the median or the variance. The parameters alone determine which alternative to choose. Although classical decision rules were at times considered mere approximations to decision rules which make use of the entire distribution,[3] they may be treated as decision rules in their own right.

The second approach has since Roy (1952) been called the 'safety first approach'. Safety first rules emphasise those results of a gamble that might or should be considered 'disastrous' by the individual. Decision rules are considered 'reasonable and probable in practice',[4] if they lead to a reduction as far as possible of the chances of a catastrophic occurrence. Thus, instead of relying on parameters alone, safety first rules utilise at least some of the information the distribution function provides on specific results and their probabilities. Such information has a special bearing in insurance mathematics. Accordingly, safety first rules had been applied to the theory of risk in insurance companies[5] some time before Roy first applied them to portfolio choice problems. Telser (1955/56) and Kataoka (1963) proposed two more safety first rules for portfolio choice settings.

Because of their emphasis on disastrous occurrences, safety first rules have always lent themselves to appeals to intuition and introspection. Their application to problems of decision under Knightian risk was thus almost always justified on rather behavioural reasoning. It might thus be argued that they should only be treated as descriptive decision rules. As such they have indeed been tested empirically, mainly in studies where behaviour under potential crisis results was analysed. But they will here be analysed also from a normative point of view, since they may be treated as normative decision rules as well.

It will become apparent in the following chapters that almost all decision rules prominent in portfolio choice theory can be attributed to the 'classical approach'. The most prominent decision rule, Markowitz's (1952) mean–variance rule, is a prime example. More recent versions of classical decision rules are also discussed. Some of these are at least influenced by safety first rules, which until recently were almost totally disregarded for portfolio choice settings. Because of their influence on recent developments, it will prove illuminating to discuss their original versions as well.

When exchanging arguments for and against decision rules used in portfolio choice theory, it will prove helpful to start with an analysis of the archetype of all decision rules, the 'expected gain rule'. It was never directly proposed for portfolio choice theory, although it is fair to say that before Markowitz founded what is now called 'modern portfolio theory' investment analysis focused solely on expected returns.[6] But this alone is no good reason for discussing the expected gain rule. What the discussion will bring forth are arguments for and against all decision rules that make use of expected values.

The same is true for the 'expected utility' principle, designed by von Neumann and Morgenstern in 1944. Their work's influence on decision theory in general and on portfolio choice theory in particular has been, and continues to be, overwhelming. Expected utility analysis has established two major lines of research. One has provided a definition of 'rational' decision making, which gained widespread acceptance, in part because of the axiomatic embedding the expected utility principle received.[7] Its influence was such that for a long time a decision rule could only be declared 'rational' by its proponents, if it complied with the expected utility's axioms. The other line of research treated the expected utility principle as descriptive, and exposed it to empirical analysis.

Serving both normative and descriptive analysis has undoubtedly contributed to its predominant role. On the other hand, its serving two masters has caused the expected utility principle to become a prime example of the continuing blurring of normative and descriptive decision theory. Discussing it will thus not only illuminate the predominant definition of 'rationality'. It will also illustrate how to separate justified from unjustified criticism. There do exist direct applications of the expected utility principle to portfolio choice theory. Friedman and Savage (1948) have used it to explain diversifying behaviour, and Tobin (1958), referring to their work, has developed a major literature on portfolio analysis. These contributions need not be analysed here in detail, as the following chapters' discussions will help explain.

3.2 EXPECTED GAIN, BERNOULLI'S MORAL EXPECTATION, AND BAYES'S RULE

A common feature of many decision rules is that mathematical expectations play an important part in them. The strong position of expected values within decision theory, and the arguments for and against their use, can best be explained by discussing decision rules that rely entirely on expected values.

The precursor of all decision rules is the expected gain rule. It was presumably the first decision rule, used in the 17th century by the French mathematician and philosopher Blaise Pascal.[8] It was also the first to be applied to games of chance and thus to decisions under Knightian risk. Many modern decision rules, like the expected utility principle, may be considered amendments to the expected gain rule, designed to overcome some of its shortcomings. Through these amendments, particularly through the expected utility principle, the expected gain rule has made its influence on portfolio choice theory felt up to the present day.

The preference index the expected gain rule assigns to a gamble is equivalent to the gamble's expected value. Omitting any index to distinguish different gambles, the preference index for any gamble is

$$\Psi(G) = \psi(E[R]) = \psi(\mu_R)$$

where R denotes the random variable having all possible results of the gamble G as its sample space.

'Result' is a general term and needs to be defined. When applied to games of chance, results are often defined as money gains, hence the decision rule's name. Results may also be defined as changes in money wealth. In portfolio choice contexts, results are commonly defined as relative changes in invested wealth, that is, percentage returns, or yields. No matter what kind of results are considered, the rule will here be called the 'expected gain rule' to avoid confusion.

Quite clearly, the expected gain rule is simple and of naive appeal. It comes as no surprise then that it has been quite popular ever since it was discussed in the 17th century. To serve as a normative decision rule, nothing is needed to support its recommendation. In the end, any normative decision rule is based on opinion and cannot be justified or refuted conclusively. The expected gain rule may thus well serve as a normative decision rule, and may be declared 'reasonable' or 'rational' just as well as any other rule.

It has, of course, quite a narrow focus. It completely disregards any aspect other than the gamble's expected value. The likelihood of achieving the expected value in a single gamble or a sequence of gambles is not contemplated. Consequences of not achieving the expected value are not evaluated. The expected value is treated as if it will occur with certainty.

It has thus been argued[9] that the expected gain rule is suitable only for decision situations in which the gambles to choose among are played an infinite number of times. In this case, long-run results may be derived from the law of large numbers. For situations of games of chance, the general form of the weak law of large numbers seems apt to be applied.[10] It states that the mean of a random sample will converge in probability to the expected value of the population. Thus, if the decision situation consists of gambles which are reiterated an infinite number of times, the gamble with the highest expected value will, with probability one, reap the highest average gain. The decision may thus be made as if the decision situation was one of certainty. Individual risk preferences, that is, subjective evaluations of the probability of other outcomes, especially of unfavourable outcomes, are rendered unnecessary. No other parameters than the expected value are needed.

The law of large numbers is thus seen as some kind of support for recommending the expected gain rule. On the other hand, it is seen as indicating its limitations. These notions have to be treated with some caution. As a normative decision rule, the expected gain rule need not be 'supported' in any way. If, of course, the law of large numbers is implicitly or explicitly used in recommending the expected gain rule, then this recommendation is limited to those decision situations to which the law of large numbers can be applied.

First, if the law of large numbers serves as some kind of support, the notion of 'plausibility' or 'rationality' is confined to situations in which the gambler is concerned solely about average gains. The convergence property stated by the law of large numbers holds only for sample averages, not for sample sums.[11]

Second, if the law of large numbers serves as some kind of support, the recommendation is also confined to situations in which the same gamble is repeated an infinite number of times.[12] If the gamble is not repeated infinitely often, the probability limits of the law of large numbers do not hold exactly. They only hold approximately. Thus, thresholds of perceptibility would have to be defined, one with respect to differences in results, and one with respect to differences in probabilities.[13] Such thresholds define which differences are still barely noticeable to the individual. They allow the determination of the number of repeats after which the result bears no noticeable difference from a result obtained after infinitely many repeats.

Unfortunately, thresholds of discernment contradict Debreu's axiom of transitivity.[14] But Debreu's axioms are any decision rule's foundation. They must be obeyed if preference indices are to express preference relations. Only under Debreu's axioms can utility functions mirror preference relations among results, or decision rules express preference relations among gambles.

Thus, if the expected gain rule's recommendation is based on the law of large numbers, it can only be called 'suitable' or 'rational' for decision situations in which the gamble is repeated infinitely often. It is then inapplicable to situations in which the gamble is played only once. It is then also inapplicable to situations in which the gamble is played only a finite number of times. Evidently, the expected gain rule is also inapplicable, if the number of repeats is prone to be restricted by forced termination. Situations of infinitely many repeats under the threat of forced premature termination lead to the problem of the gambler's ruin, which will play a major role in Chapter 4.

From a descriptive viewpoint it must be said that the expected gain rule has experienced an early and prominent empirical 'falsification', caused by its lack of subjectivity. The expected gain rule is defined in terms of the results themselves, not in terms of their utilities. It thus disregards the need to have all possible results evaluated by the decision-making individual. But preferences among gambles cannot be expressed without expressing preferences among results. The expected gain rule can thus be read as defining the results' utilities as identical to the results themselves, that is, $u(r) = r$. This implicit assumption is also found in many decision rules applied to portfolio choice problems. It implies that all individuals assign identical utilities to identical results. Results cannot be valued differently by different individuals.

This lack of subjectivity seems to be due to the expected gain rule's application to games of chance. There it might seem plausible that every individual would assign identical utilities to identical gains. It is interesting to note that the presumably first application, the 'Pari de Pascal', is not about games of chance, and Pascal does express the need for subjective evaluations.[15]

The subsequent empirical 'falsification' caused by the expected gain rule's lack of subjectivity dates back to the 18th century. Back then, the expected gain rule was the only means to evaluate games of chance. The expected value served both as the preference index of a game and the 'fair' entrance fee to a game. A game was called 'fair', if its entrance fee was equal to the expected gain of the gamble. It was simply assumed that if the entrance fee is equal to the expected value, a gamble could not favour one or the other player. Any resulting gain or loss was considered simply a matter of good or ill luck.

Accordingly, the expected gain rule's descriptive power was questioned, when a gamble was thought of to which the application of the expected gain rule failed. This gamble came to be famous as the 'St Petersburg game'. Although well known, it will briefly be described here. A single trial of the St Petersburg game consists of tossing a coin until it falls, say, 'heads'. 'Heads' first occurrence terminates the trial. The gain made in one trial depends on the number of tosses until heads first occurs. If heads occurs the first time at the kth throw, the player receives 2^{k-1} units of money. Since the probability of heads occurring for the first time at the kth throw equals 2^{-k}, the expected value of this game is an infinite series which elements are all equal to 1/2.[16] The expected value is thus infinite and it was concluded that the 'fair' entrance fee to this gamble should thus also be infinite. Nicholas Bernoulli, who first described this game in a series of letters to Raymont de Montmort, was led by mere introspection to claim that 'any fairly reasonable man' would not be willing to pay more than 20 units to participate in the game.[17] This 'empirical falsification' of the expected gain serving as the 'fair' entrance fee could not be explained, and was thus considered paradoxical.

Today, there is nothing paradoxical about the St Petersburg game. As Feller (1968) points out, modern probability theory has shown the word 'fair' to be misleading, if it is applied to gambles with infinite second moments. All that can be said about such gambles rests on the law of large numbers. All that the law of large numbers asserts is that the accumulated net gain or loss of a 'fair' gamble is likely to be of smaller magnitude than the number of times the game is played. Nothing more can be said. For gambles repeated infinitely often, this is a void statement. For gambles repeated finitely often, there is no reason to believe that the accumulated net gain fluctuates around zero. Feller provides an example where one player 'has a practical assurance' that his or her loss will exceed $n/\log n$, where n is the number of times the game is played.[18]

For the St Petersburg game, no finite expected value exists, and the law of large numbers is inapplicable. It is thus impossible to derive the 'fair' entrance fee to the St Petersburg game from the law of large numbers, on which the expected gain rule rests. It is possible to calculate entrance fees that may be called 'fair', but they do depend on the number of times the game is played, which will have to be fixed in advance.[19] This would induce an entirely different decision situation, of course, and so does not remedy the expected gain rule's inapplicability to the St Petersburg game. Today it is understood that the expected gain rule cannot serve to evaluate this game. But such considerations were unknown before mathematical rigour was introduced to probability theory.

Much of what has entered modern decision theory is closely related to alterations of the expected gain rule that have been suggested towards remedying its inapplicability to the St Petersburg game. The solution published in 1738 by Daniel Bernoulli became the most influential one.[20] Bernoulli argues that a gamble should be evaluated according to the expected value of the utilities associated with the gains, rather than according to the expected gain as such. This does remedy the lack of subjectivity mentioned above. He proposes utilities that are proportional to the gains and inversely proportional to the wealth of the gambling individual, thus arriving at a logarithmic utility function of money wealth. Bernoulli's rule thus replaces a one-to-one utility function $u(r) = r$ by a logarithmic utility function, which in the general case can be written as $u(r) = b \cdot \ln(r)$, where ln is the natural logarithm, and where b serves as a coefficient characterising the individual.

A logarithmic utility function attributes diminishing marginal utilities to money wealth, which suffices to assure us that the expected value of the utilities, the 'moral expectation' as G. Cramér calls it, is finite. Applying de l'Hôpital's rule will easily confirm this. Thus, assuming a log-utility function does suffice to remedy the expected gain rule's inapplicability to the St Petersburg game. It also remedies the lack of subjectivity, albeit only to some extent. What it does not achieve is make the rule applicable when the number of trials is finite. Bernoulli's recommendation also rests implicitly on the law of large numbers, and the law of large numbers is applicable only to situations of infinitely many reiterations.

This argument holds good for the general expected gain rule, known as Bayes's rule, which allows the use of all sorts of utility functions.[21] Bayes's rule assigns a preference index to the gambles, which equals the expected value of the utilities assigned to all possible outcomes

$$\Psi(G) = \psi(E[U]) = \psi(\mu_U)$$

with now U instead of R being the random variable considered associated with gamble G. Since no specific utility function is assumed, Bayes's rule encompasses both the expected gain rule, if $u(r) = r$, and Bernoulli's rule, if $u(r) = \ln(r)$.

What has been argued for the two special cases applies to Bayes's rule as well. As a normative rule, it may be recommended for any decision situation seen fit. But if the recommendation is based on, or implicitly supported by, the law of large numbers, it may serve as a decision rule only if the decision-making individual is concerned solely about average results, and if the gamble is played an infinite number of times. It is most important to realise that this critique holds good for all decision rules that rely on mathematical expectations.

3.3 EXPECTED UTILITY

It is no exaggeration to call the expected utility principle, or EU principle for short, the major paradigm in decision theory, and the mainstay of the analysis of behaviour under Knightian risk. It is the decision principle enjoying the most attention and the widest acceptance. Its influence has been such that it set the standard for 'rational' behaviour. For many decades it was claimed to be the only 'rational' principle and was used to evaluate the 'rationality' of all decision rules ever proposed.[22]

The EU principle was designed by von Neumann and Morgenstern (1944). According to Morgenstern, they were inspired by an article by Menger (1934) on the St Petersburg game.[23] The EU principle assigns a preference index to all gambles according to

$$\Psi(G) = \psi(E[\Phi]) = \int_{-\infty}^{\infty} \varphi(u(r))\, \mathrm{d}F(r)$$

where $u(r)$ is again a function assigning utilities to the gamble's possible results. $\varphi(u)$ is a strictly monotonically increasing function that is defined up to a linear transformation with a positive slope coefficient. It may be interpreted as capturing something like the individual's attitude towards entire gambles and their perceived 'risk'.

If $\varphi(u)$ is concave, the individual is less attracted to high utilities than deterred by low ones, yielding a decision behaviour that may be described as 'risk averse'. If $\varphi(u)$ is convex, the individual is more attracted to high utilities than deterred by low ones, yielding a behaviour that may be described as 'risk loving'. A linear $\varphi(u)$ indicates indifference towards 'risk'.

Given this property, $\varphi(u)$ is often called a 'risk preference function', but it seems that this name may lead to confusing $\varphi(u)$ with the preference index $\Psi(G)$. Here, it will be called the 'risk attitude function', which is a less ambiguous name. All in all, the preference index $\Psi(G)$ translates into the expected value of the chance variable $\Phi = \varphi(u(R))$.

Separating the functions $u(r)$ and $\varphi(u)$ is uncommon. Von Neumann and Morgenstern do not separate them. They treat $\varphi(u)$ and $u(r)$ as one single function $\omega(r)$, which they call the individual's 'utility function'. This choice of wording is rather unfortunate. $u(r)$ assigns a 'utility', that is, a preference index, to all possible results. It is thus quite different from $\omega(r)$, which combines this 'utility' with what has been called here 'risk attitude'. 'Utility' and 'risk attitude' are different concepts, and it is necessary to distinguish between them.[24] It is also more than questionable whether these two concepts can be represented by a single function. Much of Allais's (1953) critique of the EU principle rests on this point.

The necessity to distinguish between 'utility' and 'risk attitude' has led Shoemaker (1982), as well as Sugden (1986), to call $u(r)$ a 'utility function under certainty', and $\omega(r)$ a 'utility function under risk'. But this choice of wording necessitates further definitions, as well as a discussion of the relation between the two functions. Furthermore, it does not remedy the confusing use of the word 'utility'.

The concepts of 'utility' and 'risk attitude' will be distinguished here and denoted separately by the functions $u(r)$ and $\varphi(u)$. In the following, the term 'utility' will denote the individual's evaluation of possible results, unless if set in quotation marks. If set in quotations marks, 'utility' will refer to the function $\omega(r)$. The decision principle designed by von Neumann and Morgenstern will in any case be called the 'expected utility principle'.

The unfortunate lack of distinction between $\varphi(u)$ and $u(r)$ by von Neumann and Morgenstern, and their equally unfortunate choice of wording, has led to two different kinds of misinterpretation. First, it has led to claims that the EU principle was identical to Bernoulli's 'moral expectation' rule. Accordingly, it has become widespread practice, but not good practice, to call the EU principle the 'Bernoulli principle'.[25] Of course, the two are not identical at all, unless $\omega(r)$ is defined being equal to $\ln(r)$.

Second, it has led to claims that the EU principle was identical to Bayes's rule. This may be correct with regard to their mathematical form, since $u(r)$ and $\omega(r)$ are mathematically indistinguishable. But their logical content and interpretation are different, and a distinction must thus be made. Only under very special assumptions are the two identical in form and spirit. One such assumption is that the function $\varphi(u)$ is linear, that is, that the individual is neither risk averse nor risk loving.[26] But this means depriving the EU principle of much of its appeal and generality. The other such assumption is that all individuals again evaluate all possible results at face value, that is, omit the function $u(r)$ altogether by setting $u(r) = r$, which amounts to setting $\omega(r) = \varphi(u)$. But the subjective character of all decision situations of Knightian risk calls for allowing individual evaluations of results. Thus, the EU principle and Bayes's rule should not be considered equivalent. The EU principle is more general. It allows both for subjective utilities and for individual attitudes towards entire gambles. It should indeed be called a decision principle, rather than a decision rule. Until the function $\varphi(u)$ is specified, the EU principle may recommend or describe vastly different decision behaviour.

The EU principle's widespread acceptance is due to the axiomatic embedding it has received, which goes beyond the axioms of linearity, reflexivity and transitivity. These axioms provide for the existence of a general function that indicates preferences among unspecified elements of a general set. The axioms designed for the normative justification of the EU principle provide both for the existence of the risk attitude function $\varphi(u)$ and for the mathematical form of the decision principle itself.

Probably the most comprehensive system of axioms underlying the EU principle, and the most convincing discussion of them, is given by Krelle.[27] He lists eight general axioms, not all independent of each other, which he considers fundamental enough to claim that 'risk theory is hardly imaginable without them'.[28] The combination of these eight axioms with the infamous axiom of 'independent evaluation of chances', or 'independence axiom' for short, leads to the EU principle. Proponents of the EU principle will define 'rational' behaviour either as behaviour observing all of these axioms or, equivalently, as behaviour according to the EU principle.

Rationality is indeed a matter of definition. It is a fallacy to claim that Bayes's rule 'has no normative justification other than its face value, whereas [the EU principle] derives from a set of appealing decision axioms',[29] since the axioms are the logic equivalent of the EU principle. There is no difference between declaring behaviour according to a decision principle as rational and declaring behaviour according to the principle's underlying axioms as rational. Nothing but mere opinion can be brought forward to support one's view on rationality. Equivalently, nothing but mere opinion can be brought against it. Acceptance or rejection of a normative decision rule, or of one of its underlying axioms, cannot be justified conclusively.

Since 'rationality' cannot be defined conclusively, it is not surprising that part of the discussion of the EU principle's 'rationality' has turned into a discussion of its empirical validity, although this amounts to leaving the field of normative decision theory and entering that of descriptive decision theory. Although the focus of this treatise is on normative aspects, the arguments will briefly be stated here.

When discussing the empirical validity of the EU principle by testing the empirical validity of the underlying axioms, the axiom of independence has proven to be the EU principle's open flank. It may be stated as follows: Let G_1 and G_2 be two gambles, each consisting of a finite set of chances, with $G_1 \sim G_2$. Let the first k chances of both gambles be identical. If these k identical chances are substituted by a different set of k^* chances in both gambles, the preference relation $G_1 \sim G_2$ is assumed to remain valid. Put differently, if two gambles G_1 and G_2 are such that $G_1 \succ G_2$, then any convex combination $w \cdot G_1 + (1-w) \cdot G_3$ will be preferred to the convex combination $w \cdot G_2 + (1-w) \cdot G_3$ for any given value of w and any gamble G_3.

The independence axiom thus makes the individual treat all possible results independently of 'what else could happen'. This is quite a strict assumption and requirement both from a descriptive and a normative point of view. Samuelson (1952) argues that the possible results and the associated utilities are all mutually exclusive, just as the gambles between which to choose. He sees no reason why an individual's preference between two gambles should be contaminated by any third prospect with which they may be combined.

But despite this intuitive argument, experimental studies conducted, for example, by Allais (1953), Karmarkar (1974), Kahneman and Tversky (1979), Hagen (1979), McCord and de Neufville (1983) and Hershey and Shoemaker (1985), revealed decision behaviour that contradicts the independence axiom. The observed contradictions to the independence axiom in these experiments, called 'effects' rather than 'paradoxes', fall into three different categories:[30]

1. *Certainty effect and probability distortion*
   Allais has established the result that many individuals seem to give strong precedence to security over other factors. Kahneman and Tversky reported an 'overweighting of the importance' given to results associated with small probabilities.

2. *Common ratio effect*
   Let two decision situations $\{G_1, G_2\}$ and $\{G^*_1, G^*_2\}$ be designed such that the possible utility gains are the same in G_1 and G^*_1, and the same in G_2 and G^*_2. Also, let the probabilities assigned to those gains, denoted P_{G1}, P^*_{G1}, P_{G2}, and P^*_{G2}, be such that $P_{G1}/P^*_{G1} = P_{G2}/P^*_{G2}$. Then the EU principle implies that the preference relation between G_1 and G_2 must be the same as between G^*_1 and G^*_2. This, however, was not the case for the majority of all individuals observed by Kahneman and Tversky and by Hagen.

3. *Utility evaluation effect*
   Empirical observations gathered by Allais, Karmarkar, and by McCord and de Neufville indicate that many individuals do not express preferences among gambles according to functions that are linear in $\varphi(u(r))$. The value of the function $\varphi(u(r))$ seems not to depend on $u(r)$ alone, but to increase with increasing probability of r.

All these effects, which have been frequently observed, constitute systematic empirical violations of the EU principle. Despite Samuelson's intuitive argument, the EU principle cannot serve as a descriptive decision principle.

Although its normative position cannot be harmed by any of the effects found, further research took a descriptive stand and tried to reconcile the EU principle with the empirical findings. Among them are Machina's (1982) 'generalised expected utility' model, 'distortion' models, like Yaari's (1987) 'dual choice' model, and a similar model by Allais (1987). There are, furthermore, a number of models employing different mathematical formulations of the function $\varphi(u(r))$, like Hagen's (1979) 'three moments' model, or like 'regret theory', which has simultaneously been proposed by Bell (1982), Loomes and Sudgen (1982) and Fishburn (1982). More recently, a number of explanations for the violation of the independence axiom have been proposed, which have been dubbed 'similarity' models. Their explanation rests on bounded and costly rationality, with the evaluation costs depending on the 'similarity' between the prospects. These models are connected with names like Rubinstein (1988), Leland (1990), Buschena (1992) and Buschena and Zilberman (1994a).

These extensions will not be described in detail here.[31] The EU principle has been discussed because it has entered portfolio choice theory as a yardstick for rationality. As has been argued, no compelling reasons can be given to necessarily accept it as such. In addition, empirical findings have weakened the position of the EU principle, but this is not the main point here. The main point is that the argument brought against the use of any decision rule employing expected values also applies to the EU principle, because the latter assigns a preference index to all gambles that is equivalent to the expected value of the chance variable $\Phi = \varphi(u(R))$. There is no fundamental difference between the preference indices $E[R]$, $E[u(R)]$ and $E[\varphi(u(R)]$. They are all expected values. The only difference between these preference indices is that different results are associated with the gamble G. This argument also holds good for all the above listed amendments to the EU principle, which is why they need not be described in detail here.[32]

Again, the argument is that if an expected value has been recommended under explicit or implicit reference to the law of large numbers, then this recommendation can be considered applicable only if the individual is concerned solely about average results, and if the gamble is repeated an infinite number of times. Only if the gamble is repeated an infinite number of times can the law of large numbers assure that the long-run average result will lie arbitrarily close to the expected value. In this case, the expected value can indeed serve as an indicator of 'what to expect' and may be used to indicate the individual's preference among the gambles. If the gambles are not repeated an infinite number of times, the expected value may be a very poor indicator of the actual outcome.

This is not sufficient reason to reject it as a normative decision rule in every case, since normative decision rules cannot be evaluated conclusively. But if the EU principle finds explicit or implicit support in the law of large numbers, it is only applicable to situations of Knightian risk where infinite repeats are feasible.

It is not unjustified to claim that the EU principle does seek implicit or explicit support in the law of large numbers. After all, von Neumann and Morgenstern were influenced by Menger's article on the St Petersburg paradox and by Bernoulli's proposed solution to it. As has already been argued, Bernoulli's solution rests implicitly on the law of large numbers, and thus on infinitely many repeats. The St Petersburg paradox is about a game of chance, where infinitely many repeats are conceivable. Since the EU principle has been designed against this background, an implicit reference to infinitely many repeats would not be surprising.

This opinion is shared by many. For example, Roy (1952) claims that the EU principle is 'only rational if the individuals are free to expose themselves to independent risks on a large number of occasions'.[33] It is thus questionable whether the EU principle's widespread acceptance is only due to the axiomatic embedding it received. Its acceptance has almost certainly been boosted by the fact that it is simply an expected value, similar in kind to and thus reminiscent of both the expected gain rule and Bernoulli's moral expectation rule. If so, the support the law of large numbers lends to the expected gain rule has implicitly been applied to the EU principle as well. The EU principle is then not an adequate preference index for gambles that are played only a finite number of times, or for gambles that are prone to forced premature termination.

Again, this is not to say that the EU principle may not be claimed as 'rational' in other decision situations. 'Rationality' is a matter of opinion and cannot be disputed. What is argued here is that the predominance of expected values in decision theory, and especially in decision rules for portfolio choice problems, can be explained by decision theory's history of thought. The first decision rules were expected values, applied to games of chance in settings of infinitely many repeats, and supported by a notion that was to become the law of large numbers. The support the first decision rules found in the law of large numbers is implicitly passed on to any decision rule employing expected values, including the EU principle. Only in settings of infinitely many repeats does recommending the EU principle find support beyond the statement that it is 'rational'.

This point also raises serious objections against trying to reconcile any decision principle with the EU principle. As soon as a decision principle is defined such that it becomes a special case of the EU principle, infinitely many repeats are necessary to support it. This point also applies to the most renowned decision rule used in portfolio choice theory, Markowitz's (1952) μ–σ^2 rule, which has been forced by Markowitz and many other authors to submit itself under the EU principle.

3.4 MARKOWITZ'S μ–σ^2 RULE

μ–σ^2 rules fall into the category of 'classical' decision rules. Classical decision rules do not utilise all the information that is provided by the distributions of the random variables related to a gamble. They assign a preference index that is a function of only one or several parameters of the distributions. This confinement was originally justified by regarding classical decision rules as approximations to such rules that are based on the entire distribution.[34]

μ–σ^2 rules assign a preference index to all gambles according to some function of the expected value and the variance of the chance variables R or U

$$\Psi(G) = \psi(E[R], V[R]) = \psi(\mu_R, \sigma_R^2)$$

To be operational, the function $\psi(.)$ needs to be specified. Freund (1956) uses a function that is linear in μ_R and σ_R^2. Thomas (1958) uses a function that is linear in μ_R and σ_R.

The μ–σ^2 rules' standing within portfolio choice theory is due to Markowitz (1952). Markowitz's μ–σ^2 rule may be considered the mainstay of decision rules in portfolio choice theory, just as the EU principle may be considered the mainstay of decision theory. Although Markowitz was neither the first nor the only one to treat portfolio choice problems as decisions under Knightian risk, his analysis had nevertheless the greatest influence on all subsequent modern portfolio and finance theories. Not a few cite his work as having laid the foundations of modern investment theory.

Several reasons may be given for this overwhelming impact. First, Markowitz adapts his μ–σ^2 rule to investment problems by defining the gambles' results as percentage returns, or 'yields'. Second, he interprets the expected value and variance of the returns in a way that appeals to intuition.

By using percentage returns, Markowitz acknowledges that investment decisions are of a different nature than decisions concerning games of chance. Investment decisions have an inherent time dimension that needs to be considered, whereas the time needed to play one game of chance is rather irrelevant. Decision rules applicable to investment problems must thus treat money gains made over different periods of time as different results. They are of different value, because they allow consumption at different points in time.[35] In consumption and investment theory, connecting different points in time is the task of interest rates.

Accordingly, the possible results of an investment decision must be stated in percentage returns, or yields, rather than in absolute gains. Returns, defined in continuous time space as

$$r = \frac{(\mathrm{d}w/\mathrm{d}t)}{w}$$

with w being the amount of money invested, explicitly introduce the time dimension. The parameters used by Markowitz are thus the expected value and the variance of an investment's percentage returns.

The intuitively appealing interpretations that Markowitz provides for the expected value and the variance had an even bigger impact. He suggests treating the 'expected value' of the returns as the 'return to expect', although not without pointing at the imperfect relation between the two terms.[36] This interpretation goes beyond the one that rests on the law of large numbers. Markowitz does not recommend using the expected value by referring to infinitely many repeats. He recommends using it as a forecast of the investment's return. Being concerned about uncertain future events, investors should be looking for some forecasting method to guide their decisions. Using the expected value is such a method.

Markowitz does not view the expected value as the result that will occur with certainty. Thus, a measure is needed of how likely returns other than the expected value are, and how much confidence an investor may thus have in the guiding quality of the expected value. Markowitz interprets the variance of the returns as such a measure. More specifically, he interprets the variance as a measure of the possibility of unfavourable results.

This may be justifiable, at least for some decision situations. If the situation is characterised by normally distributed gambles, variance and standard deviation may well be used to calculate probabilities and confidence ranges for results around the expected value. Markowitz thus declares the variance to be a direct measure of the 'risk' involved in investment decisions. This insinuates that 'risk' was measurable by a single statistical entity. 'Risk' thus turns from an undefined characteristic of a decision situation into something inherently tangible and tractable. Expected value and variance become siblings. One sibling serves as an indicator for which 'return to expect' on the investment, the other sibling serves as an indicator for the 'risk' inherent in it.

The intuitive appeal of this dichotomy into 'return' and 'risk' has proven irresistible. It has become so influential that many alternatives proposed to Markowitz's rule are mainly concerned with what statistical entity to use instead of the variance as the measure for 'risk'.

The use of expected values and variances brought along some presentational ease. Portfolio returns, their expected value and their variance, may easily be calculated from the returns of single assets, their expected values and their variances and covariances. This results from two basic theorems of mathematical statistics. Every conceivable portfolio may thus easily be included in the decision process, without knowledge of the entire distribution of its returns.

The decision process can also conveniently be separated into two steps. First, the portfolios with the highest expected value for given levels of variance are calculated. Second, the portfolio valued highest according to the individual's decision rule is selected. Since this two-step approach will prove helpful in comparing all decision rules that will be discussed in the following, it will be described here in some detail using graphical tools.[37]

The set of gambles to choose among in a situation of portfolio choice is given by the set of all assets in which an individual can invest and all their possible combinations. Markowitz calls this the 'attainable set',[38] nowadays more commonly referred to as the 'feasible set' or the 'opportunity set'. Each investment and each portfolio are identified by the μ–σ^2 combination it offers, these being the only characteristics that matter to the individual.

The first step in solving the portfolio choice problem is to identify the set of portfolios that render the highest value of μ for a given value of σ^2. Mathematically this is done by optimising the Lagrangean function

$$L(\mathbf{x},\lambda_1,\lambda_2) = \mathbf{x}'\,\Sigma\mathbf{x} - \lambda_1 \cdot(\mathbf{x}'\mu - k) - \lambda_2\cdot(\mathbf{s}'\mathbf{x} - 1)$$

for the weights x_h, where $\mathbf{x}$ is the column vector of weights, Σ is the matrix of variances and covariances of the assets' returns, μ is the column vector of the returns' expected values, $\mathbf{s}$ is a summer vector and k is the fixed required expected value. This optimisation will yield the boundary of the feasible set. Under the assumption that investors are generally risk averse, together with some further conditions,[39] this boundary is shaped in (μ, σ) space as depicted in Figure 3.1. (μ, σ) space may be chosen for presentational ease without further precautions, because of the one-to-one relationship between variance and standard deviation.

Within the feasible set, which includes the boundary, lie all feasible investments, that is, all single assets and all possible portfolios. The 'efficient set' is the set of assets and portfolios offering the lowest standard deviation for a given level of expected value, or, equivalently, the set of assets and portfolios offering the highest expected value for a given level of standard deviation. It is depicted as that part of the boundary that lies between points *A* and *B*, with *A* being the 'minimum variance portfolio'.

The boundary of the feasible set does not simply connect those assets that offer superior expected value-to-variance ratios. The most important result of the optimisation procedure is that broadly diversified portfolios

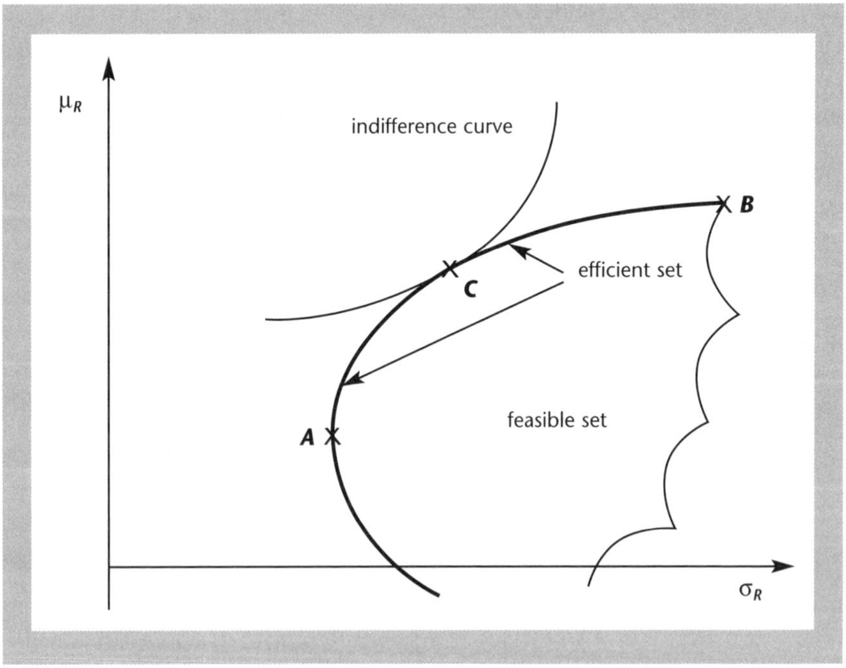

Figure 3.1 Portfolio choice in Markowitz's model

offer better risk–return ratios than the single assets of the feasible set. This is so because the expected value of a sum of random variables is a linear combination of the random variables' expected values, whereas the standard deviation of a sum of random variables is smaller than the linear combination of the random variables' standard deviations. This is due to the covariances involved, and true unless all correlation coefficients are equal to one.

After having identified the efficient set, the second step is to choose among the portfolios of the 'efficient set'. The portfolio with the highest preference value is the most preferred one, which can be mathematically determined by optimising the preference index that is given by the decision rule.

Graphically the most preferred portfolio can be determined with the help of indifference curves. Portfolios that are attributed equal preference values are indifferent to the investor, and sets of indifferent portfolios will form an indifference curve that may by drawn in (μ, σ) space. Under the assumption that the investor accepts, or is recommended to accept, higher standard deviations only in return for higher expected returns, such indifference curves will form a convex line in (μ, σ) space.[40] The most preferred portfolio can then be identified by the coordinates of that point of the efficient set where an indifference curve is tangent to it. In Figure 3.1 the most preferred portfolio is identified as point *C*.

Because the efficient set consists of broadly diversified portfolios, investors behaving according to Markowitz's μ–σ^2 rule prefer in almost all cases to diversify their wealth.[41] Diversification of investments, that is, holding portfolios rather than single assets, is a superior investment strategy, because it yields more preferred expected value-to-variance opportunities. This result, together with all the convenience the μ–σ^2 analysis provides, is the reason for the μ–σ^2 rule's success and high standing within portfolio choice theory. Indeed, diversification behaviour cannot only be observed, which renders some empirical justification for Markowitz's work, it seems almost 'irrational' not to diversify under normal circumstances. Any normative decision rule that fails to recommend diversification in common situations will be difficult to label 'rational'.[42] The recommendation and explanation of diversification behaviour can be considered an acid test for any decision rule that is to be applied to portfolio choice theory. This will be remembered when alternative decision rules are proposed.

A modification to Markowitz's model, proposed by Tobin (1958, 1965), includes a single riskless asset, that is, an asset with $V[R] = 0$. With such an asset the shape of the efficient set changes from concave to linear. This can be shown mathematically by applying the same optimisation procedure as above. But the efficient set in case a risk-free asset exists can also be constructed graphically from Markowitz's model. This is done in Figure 3.2. The relation between the two models then becomes apparent.

The concave curve is again the boundary of the feasible set of investments, if no 'risk-free' asset exists. To avoid confusion it will be called the 'feasible set of all risky investments'. If a risk-free asset exists, the feasible set is constructed by drawing two lines emanating from the point (r_f, 0), the risk–return combination of the risk-free asset. These lines must be a tangent to the border of the feasible set of all risky investments, because of the optimisation procedure. Tobin imposes the non-negativity constraint $x_h \geq 0$ on all assets except for the risk-free one, which amounts to assuming that funds may be borrowed at a cost equal to the risk-free rate. The rays emanating from the point (r_f, 0) are thus unbounded to the right.

The efficient set of Tobin's model is given by the upper ray in Figure 3.2, since only those portfolios offering the highest expected value for

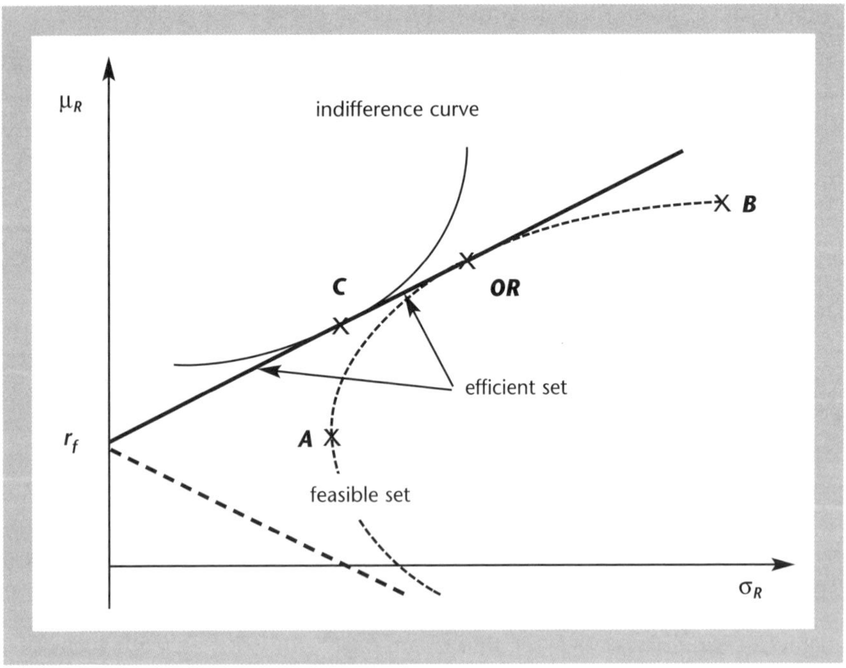

Figure 3.2 Portfolio choice in Tobin's model

any given level of variance are 'efficient'. This efficient set consists of combinations of the risk-free asset with the tangent 'risky' portfolio of the efficient set of Markowitz's model. All investors will choose portfolios that are linear combinations of the risk-free asset and the optimal risky portfolio, which is denoted *OR* in Figure 3.2. Every investor chooses *OR* as his or her 'risky' portfolio. Which portfolio is chosen as the optimal overall portfolio, depends on the individual's decision rule, which can again be depicted by an indifference curve. The indifference curve drawn in Figure 3.2 indicates one such decision made, again denoted portfolio *C*.

Another refinement of Markowitz's model is made by Black (1972), who removes the non-negativity constraint $x_h \geq 0 \; \forall \; h$ on the assets' weights, but does not assume that a risk-free asset exists. In this case, the 'efficient set' assumes the shape of the upper part of a parabola in (μ, σ^2) space, and of a hyperbola in (μ, σ) space.[43] Both the parabola and the hyperbola lie parallel to the horizontal axis. The efficient set can thus be described using the known mathematical formulae for these geometric figures. The vertex of the hyperbola is equivalent to the minimum variance portfolio. If a risk-free asset is assumed to exist, the efficient set is given by the equivalent asymptote of the hyperbola. Further refinements were introduced, for example by Brennan (1971) or Dyl (1975). Since the decision rule remains unaltered in any refinements of Markowitz's model, they need not be described in detail here.

Markowitz's rule can be discussed both from a normative and a descriptive point of view. Markowitz himself considers it both normative and descriptive.[44] He thus undoubtedly contributed to the unfortunate blurring between normative and descriptive perspectives in portfolio choice theory. Since the focus of this treatise is on normative decision rules, the empirical validity of Markowitz's μ–σ^2 rule will not be discussed in detail. It may be noted, though, that Markowitz disregards the subjective character of all decision rules. He disregards the need to have all results evaluated by the individual, who must assign utilities to the returns before he or she can make any decision.

Accordingly, Markowitz treats the decision as among the return distributions of all conceivable portfolios, that is, among the random variables R_i, not among the random variables U_i. Since a subjective evaluation is necessary, it must be concluded that Markowitz supposes that all individuals evaluate percentage returns at face value, that is, $u(r) = r$.

It is interesting to note, although not surprising, that $u(r) = r$ is equivalent to presuming a logarithmic utility function of monetary wealth. As has been noted when discussing Bernoulli's rule in section 3.2, a logarithmic utility function of monetary wealth implies diminishing marginal utilities of monetary wealth.[45] That monetary wealth has diminishing marginal utilities is sometimes disputed. On the other hand, Markowitz's μ–σ^2 rule explains observable diversification behaviour well, and some empirical validity may therefore be granted.

Any normative discussion of Markowitz's μ–σ^2 rule has for a very long time been influenced by the EU principle's definition of rationality. Being the prevalent definition of rationality at the time, even Markowitz desired to reconcile his rule with the EU principle.[46] It has turned out that any μ–σ^2 rule may in fact be regarded a special case of the EU principle. This result is usually derived using the compound notation of the EU principle, that is, $\Psi(G) = E[\omega(R)]$, instead of $\Psi(G) = E[\varphi(u(R))]$. When the utility function u(.) and the risk attitude function φ(.) are kept separate, the argument runs as follows.[47] There exists a theorem which states that a classical decision principle $\Psi(G) = \psi(\alpha_1, \alpha_2, ..., \alpha_K)$, with the α_k being mathematical expectations of some functions of the values $u(r) = u$ of the random variable U, that is, $\alpha_k = E[h_k(U)]$, is a special case of the EU principle if and only if (1) the risk attitude function is linear in the $h_k(u)$

$$\varphi(u) = a_0 + \sum_{k=1}^{K} a_k \cdot h_k(u)$$

and if therefore (2) the classical principle is linear in the $E[h_k(U)]$

$$\Psi(G) = \psi(\alpha_1, \alpha_2, ..., \alpha_K) = a_0 + \sum_{k=1}^{K} a_k \cdot \alpha_k = a_0 + \sum_{k=1}^{K} a_k \cdot E[h_k(U)] \quad .$$

Here, a possible monotonic transformation has been disregarded.

Clearly, all that is said by this theorem relates only to the risk attitude function $\varphi(u)$, not to the compound function $\omega(r)$. Also, Markowitz's μ–σ^2 rule defines $u(r) = r$, yielding for the EU principle $\Psi(G) = E[\omega(R)] = E[\varphi(R)]$, and the functions $h_k(u)$ become $h_k(r)$. The a_k's thus become expected values of some transformation of the chance variable R. For Markowitz's rule, μ equals $E[R]$ and thus $\alpha_1 = E[R]$ with $h_1(r) = r$. σ^2 equals $E[R^2] - E^2[R]$, where the first term yields $\alpha_2 = E[R^2]$ with $h_2(r) = r^2$. The second term, $E^2[R]$, must not appear in $\psi(\alpha_1, \alpha_2, ..., \alpha_K)$ according to the above theorem, since it is quadratic and not linear. If σ^2 is wanted in the decision rule, $E^2[R]$ has to be neutralised by simply adding it again. Thus, if Markowitz's μ–σ^2 rule is forced to submit itself under the EU principle, it has to be of the form

$$\psi(G) = \psi(\alpha_1, \alpha_2) = \psi(\mu, \sigma^2) = a_0 + a_1 \cdot \mu + a_2 \cdot \sigma^2 + a_2 \cdot \mu^2$$

and the risk attitude function of the equivalent EU principle is then of the form

$$\varphi(u) = \varphi(r) = a_0 + a_1 \cdot r + a_2 \cdot r^2$$

Since monotonic transformations are possible, the constant may be set equal to zero, and the coefficient a_2 may be reduced to ±1 by multiplication with an appropriate factor.

According to the above theorem, the decision rule proposed by Markowitz is 'rational', as defined by the EU principle, only if it is of the form given above. Equivalently, if an EU rule is to be chosen that is equivalent to Markowitz's μ–σ^2 rule, this EU rule's risk attitude function has to be quadratic in the returns.[48] This quadratic form does seem implausible, as has repeatedly been remarked. It leads to a reversal in the evaluation of the chances of a risky prospect, beginning at some threshold return. Markowitz argues in turn that only one side of the function $\varphi(r)$ should be considered, assuming distributions of R that are bounded by some value.[49] If so, every function may be approximated by one side of a parabola. But this does presuppose investors that are either risk averse or risk loving. No risk attitude function can be approximated that displays both areas of decreasing and of increasing slope.

The quadratic risk attitude function is only then a necessary consequence of the above-stated theorem, if the μ–σ^2 rule is to be applied to gambles where the distribution of the results is unspecified. If decision situations are taken as a choice among distributions that are identified by their expected value and their variance alone, no implausible restrictions on the risk attitude functions are needed. This is the case for the class of normal distributions and the class of log-normal distributions. It has thus been concluded that mean–variance rules are 'rational' only either if quadratic risk attitude functions or if special probability distributions are involved.[50] Up to the present day, any discussion of Markowitz's μ–σ^2 rule includes this conclusion on its 'rationality'.

It seems worth emphasising that this entire argument is based on declaring the EU principle the only 'rational' one. It is true that there has been a time when the von Neumann–Morgenstern definition of rationality was irrefutable; and most works on the relationship of the EU principle and Markowitz's μ–σ^2 rule stem from this time. But, as has been argued in section 2.2, the EU principle's claim to absolute right cannot be maintained. Normative considerations on the 'rationality' of decision rules are a matter of mere opinion. Rationality cannot be defined conclusively. There is thus no need to reconcile any decision rule with the EU principle. Different axiomatic systems may be designed to define rationality.

A system of axioms is not even necessary, due to the logical equivalence of a decision rule with its underlying axioms. A decision rule may simply be defined as 'rational' without having recourse to an axiomatic underpinning, that is, without trying to embed it in a system of axioms. An axiomatic system might help to support one's opinion on rational behaviour, but rational behaviour may as well be defined directly by declaring a decision rule as rational. Krelle discusses an alternative to the EU principle that does not rely on the independence axiom.[51] He discards the independence axiom, proposes a rule that is a function of the expected value and the mean absolute diversion of the gamble's results, and simply declares it 'rational'. He abstains from embedding it in an alternative set of axioms, stating that no set of axioms he created is simpler or more evident than the decision principle itself.

It must thus be stated that no compelling reasons can be given to refute Markowitz's decision rule on normative grounds. His decision rule may be as 'rational' as any other, depending on the adopted definition of 'rationality'. What can be said is that Markowitz's decision rule also rests, albeit indirectly, on the law of large numbers.

In addition to employing the expected value of the returns and in addition to measuring 'risk' by the variance, which is just another expected value, Markowitz's decision rule also relies indirectly on the law of large numbers because of his justification for using expected values. Markowitz proposes treating the expected value as the 'return to expect', thus referring to the predominant problem any individual is confronted with in situations under Knightian risk. 'What to expect' when facing a random variable is a problem of prediction.

The problem of prediction is the main feature of all decisions under Knightian risk. That a decision has to be made is not the main feature. Decisions must also be made in decision situations under certainty. The main feature is that the result of the action taken is uncertain. Thus, a need arises to predict the uncertain result. Of course, if infinitely often repeated gambles are considered, the problem of prediction may be resolved by turning to the law of large numbers. It renders results that carry probability one. The link between decisions under Knightian risk and the problem of prediction is thus not self-evident, if infinitely often repeated gambles are in the back of one's mind.

But in the case of investment decisions and problems of portfolio choice, an infinite repetition of the same investment is not the rule. The need to predict the result of an investment is thus inherent. The choice of which parameters to include in any decision rule applied to portfolio choice problems, be it normative or descriptive, may thus be governed by their predictive qualities. That is the implicit reasoning given by Markowitz for choosing the expected value.

Unfortunately, combining the expected value with the variance also renders his decision rule plausible only for infinitely often repeated gambles. It can easily be shown that the expected value of a random variable is the predictor of choice if the criterion for good prediction, or the cost measure of false prediction, is the mean squared forecast error, or MSFE for short.[52] If c is the quantity chosen to predict the next value the random variable Y will take on, the MSFE is defined as $E[(Y-c)^2]$. The value that minimises the MSFE is the expected value $E[Y]$. The MSFE is a criterion for predictive success that is widespread in statistics and econometrics. Classical econometrics is concerned with estimating the conditional expectation function $E[Y|\mathbf{X}]$, with $\mathbf{X}$ being a random vector, because it is the best predictor in the multivariate case as judged by the MSFE. The minimum value of the MSFE in the univariate case is equal to the variance of Y, since $\min E[(Y-c)^2] = E[(Y-E[Y])^2] = V[Y]$, which is the parameter proposed by Markowitz as the measure of the risk of an investment.

Markowitz's choice of parameters can thus be given two somewhat different but related interpretations. The expected value $E[R]$ is not only an indicator or the central tendency of the return's distribution. It is also the best constant predictor of the chance experiment's next outcome, if minimising the MSFE is the criterion of choice. The variance $V[R]$, chosen by Markowitz as a measure of the 'risk' of an investment, is not only an indicator of the distribution's dispersion around the expected value. It is also a measure of the precision of repeated forecasts. If forecast errors were to be punished according to the sum of their realised squared deviations, the expected value $E[R]$ would minimise the expectation of this punishment to the value $E[(R-E[R])^2] = V[R]$. The choice of the parameters $E[R]$ and $V[R]$, which seems somewhat arbitrary when judged by decision theory standards alone,[53] is anything but arbitrary in light of the problem of prediction. Combining the expected value and the variance is compulsive, when accepting the MSFE as the criterion for forecasting quality. Keeping in mind that problems of prediction are inherent in problems of decision under Knightian risk, combining the two parameters into one decision rule is thus more than plausible.

But it is plausible only if the investment is repeated an infinite number of times, since underneath Markowitz's decision rule lies the expected value of the random variable $(R - E[R])^2$. Infinitely many repeats are required to ensure that the expected value of this random variable will be realised, that is, that the average of the realised squared forecast errors will be of minimum value, and thus that the risk involved in investing is adequately described by the variance of the returns. Thus, when viewed in combination with the problem of forecasting, Markowitz's decision rule is clearly suitable only in situations of infinitely many repeats.

3.5 SAFETY FIRST RULES

Safety first rules may be considered special cases of classical decision rules, but they deserve a separate treatment because of their special emphasis on some of the gambles' possible results. Safety first rules assume that decision makers should be, or indeed are, concerned with avoiding such results of their action that they consider distinctly unfavourable.

Examples of such unfavourable results found in the literature are usually of rather catastrophic, even morbid nature. They include shipwreck, bankruptcy, imprisonment, ambush, starvation and death sentence. Bankruptcy is the most prominent example, especially in the form of insolvency of insurance companies, because safety first rules have for some time been the mainstay of insurance mathematics, that is, theories of risk of insurance companies.[54] But there is no need to associate total disaster with the term 'unfavourable result'. Certainly the above are examples of events that almost every individual would consider 'unfavourable'. But in portfolio choice theory, an individual may consider results other than a complete loss of the sum invested distinctly unfavourable, depending on his or her situation.

Safety first rules have experienced a varied history in portfolio choice theory. Roy (1952) published a treatise on portfolio choice based on a very simple safety first rule at very much the same time as Markowitz published his μ–σ^2 based theory. But Markowitz's ideas overshadowed Roy's from the very beginning. This may have been due to several facts. First, Markowitz's μ–σ^2 rule has more intuitive appeal. Second, Roy's decision rule leads to rather implausible diversification behaviour in some situations, while Markowitz's rule is applicable more generally. Third, Markowitz accepts the EU principle's definition of rationality, the prevailing opinion of the time, and subsequently reconciles his decision principle with it. Roy refutes the EU principle in his article,[55] and has to acknowledge that a rather implausible risk attitude function is required to make his decision rule congruent with it.[56]

The ground Roy lost from the very beginning could not be recovered by Telser (1955/56) and Kataoka (1963), although they designed their rules to remedy some of the shortcomings of Roy's safety first rule. To put it briefly, safety first rules never played a significant role in portfolio choice theory.

But some of the ideas of Roy, Telser and Kataoka, if not their decision rules, have lately re-entered portfolio choice theory in the wake of the criticism brought against Markowitz's μ–σ^2 rule. Markowitz's interpretation of the variance as a measure of the 'risk' of an investment is refuted on rather descriptive considerations and substituted by something now commonly called 'downside risk'.[57] One quantification of 'downside risk' is the 'shortfall probability', which is in fact simply the probability of the return falling below some predetermined level. Since Roy's decision rule translates into a proposal to minimise this 'shortfall probability', he has regained, in part at least, consideration in modern portfolio choice theory. Also, combining the expected value with the probability of the return falling short of some level is very close to what Telser and Kataoka propose.

All these more recent developments in portfolio choice theory will be discussed in section 3.6. In this chapter, the rules of Roy, Telser and Kataoka are discussed for two reasons. First, because of the influence they had on more recent developments, and second, because they are based on probabilities. Their analysis will be helpful because probabilities play an important role in the decision rules proposed in Chapter 4.

Roy's (1952) safety first rule assigns a preference index to all gambles according to their probability of rendering a result above some predetermined level d^*. For the continuous case, and taking returns as results, his rule may be stated as

$$\Psi(G) = P(R = r > d^*) = \int_{d^*}^{\infty} f(r)\,\mathrm{d}r$$

Again, the gamble with the highest index is chosen. Maximising $P(R = r > d^*)$ is, of course, equivalent to minimising $P(R = r \leq d^*)$.

It may first be noted that any subjective evaluation of the possible results is again missing. Subjectivity is provided for only by the individual's choice of the value d^*. This could, of course, easily be remedied by exchanging utilities assigned to the results for the results themselves.

No critique against his normative ideal can be raised. Roy expresses his idea of rational behaviour by claiming it to be 'reasonable' for those who have some such idea of disaster 'to seek to reduce as far as is possible the chance of such a catastrophe occurring'.[58] Such a definition of 'rationality' cannot be refuted, as has repeatedly been argued here.

Of course, judged by the EU principle's definition of rationality, Roy's rule is rather implausible. According to the theorem given in section 3.4, a classical decision rule is a special case of the EU principle if and only if (1) the risk attitude function it implies is linear in $h_k(u)$, and (2) the decision rule is linear in $\alpha_k = E[h_k(U)]$. Roy's decision rule comprises only one quantity, $P(R = r > d^*)$, which translates into an expected value of the above kind only if $u(r) = r$, and if

$$h(r) = \begin{cases} 0 & \text{if } r \leq d^* \\ 1 & \text{if } r > d^* \end{cases}$$

Then, $\alpha = E[h(U)]$, and the risk attitude function becomes

$$\varphi(u(r)) = \varphi(r) = \begin{cases} a_0 & \text{if } r \leq d^* \\ a_0 + a_1 & \text{if } r > d^* \end{cases}$$

This risk attitude function distinguishes only two kinds of results. Those that are higher than the disaster level and those that are lower or equal to it. The former receive a ranking which is higher by a summand a_1, no matter how far away they lie from the disaster level or any parameter of central tendency.

The risk attitude function also displays a discontinuity, which has been criticised by proponents of the EU principle.[59] Some authors have even used a set of axioms for the EU principle that rules out such discontinuities.[60] But Roy claims that 'there would appear to be no valid objection to the discontinuity in the preference scale that the existence of a single disaster value implies',[61] thus again expressing his opinion on rationality.

Again, it must be remembered that any reconciliation with the EU principle is both unnecessary and counterproductive. It is unnecessary, because the EU principle's definition of rationality is not omnipotent. It is counterproductive, because the EU principle gathers and provides additional support only in situations of infinitely many repeats.

Serious objections against Roy's safety first rule may be raised from a different point of view. The probability $P(R = r \leq d^*)$ is the only parameter that guides any decision. No other parameter is included in the preference function ψ. Thus, Roy's decision rule does not weigh the risk of a investment against the possible gains, which could be measured by another parameter. He does admit that the value d^* may not be independent of any such parameter, as, for instance, the expected value. But he altogether disregards the possibility of an individual being willing to accept a higher probability for the event $\{R = r \leq d^*\}$ in exchange for higher possible gains.

The consequence is that the portfolio choices the rule suggests seem rather implausible in some situations. Diversification is recommended or explained only if the existence of a risk-free asset is excluded. If a risk-free asset exists, and if it yields a return above the level d^*, an individual acting according to Roy's safety first rule will not diversify but will invest all of his or her wealth in the risk-free asset. In contrast, Markowitz's μ–σ^2 rule recommends diversification, whether or not a risk-free asset is assumed to exist.[62]

The recommendations Roy's rule makes can easily be shown graphically by having recourse to Chebyshev's inequality, which can be used to calculate an upper bound for $P(R = r \leq d^*)$. Chebyshev's inequality yields

$$P\left(R = r \leq d^*\right) \leq \frac{V[R]}{\left(E[R] - d^*\right)^2}$$

Minimising $P(R = r \leq d^*)$ is then obviously equivalent to maximising $(\mu_R - d^*)/\sigma_R$, and Roy's rule turns into a classical μ–σ rule with $\psi(\mu_R, \sigma_R) = (\mu_R - d^*)/\sigma_R$.[63] Chebyshev's inequality thus allows the depiction and analysis of Roy's rule in (μ, σ) space.

It also allows a separation of the analysis into two steps. The first step, the identification of the 'efficient set', is the same as in Markowitz's model of portfolio choice. In both cases the determination of the most preferred portfolio starts with the optimisation procedure that constructs the 'efficient set'. Since Roy implicitly excludes a risk-free asset and negative weights, his 'efficient set' has the same shape as Markowitz's. The set is depicted in Figure 3.3.

According to Roy's decision rule, the most preferred portfolio is determined graphically by drawing a straight line of positive slope, emanating from point $(0, d^*)$, that is a tangent to the efficient set. The steeper the slope of this line, the less probable a return less than d^*, since the upper bound of the probability of disaster is equal to the reciprocal of the square of the line's gradient.[64] Which portfolio is preferred thus depends

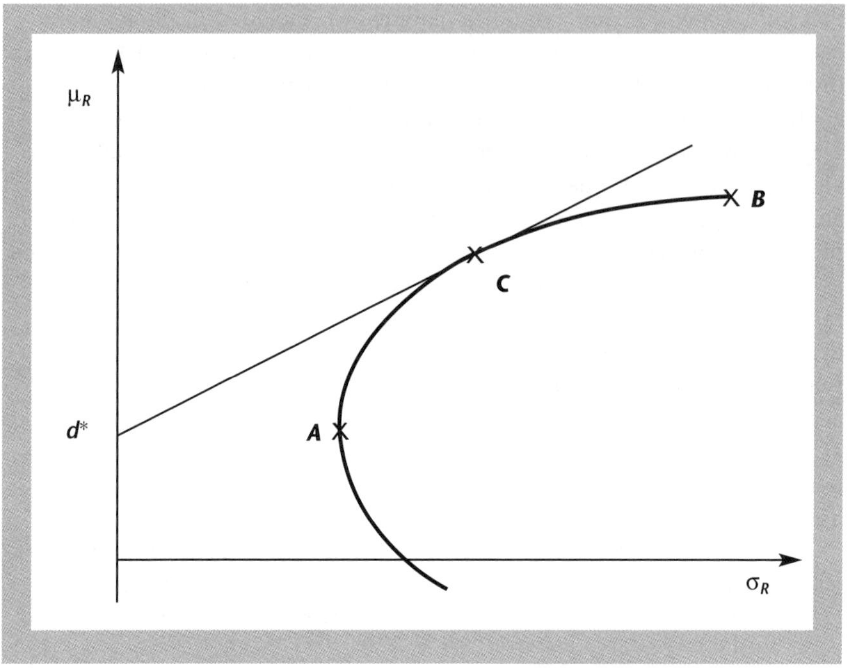

Figure 3.3 Portfolio choice in Roy's model

only on d^*. The consequence is that the closer the investor's preferred portfolio lies to the minimum-variance portfolio, the lower the level d^* he or she sees as disastrous. In other words, the less worried an individual is about disastrous results, the less variation in returns he or she tolerates. This seems peculiar. One would expect that the less worried an individual is, the more 'risky' a portfolio he or she may be recommended to choose. But this peculiarity is explained when it is remembered that the level d^* does not indicate any risk preference. The only value that enters the risk preference function is $P(R = r \leq d^*)$, which is always minimised no matter what value d^* indicates disaster in a given situation.

Another consequence of this single-parameter decision rule is that it fails to recommend or explain diversification behaviour, if a risk-free return is achievable. This is indicated in Figure 3.4. As explained in section 3.4, the shape of the efficient set changes from concave to linear when an asset with $V[R] = 0$ is included. Given such an efficient set, and if $d^* < r_f$, an individual acting according to Roy's decision rule will invest all wealth in the risk-free asset. If $d^* > r_f$, the individual would either invest all in portfolio *OR*, or, if the non-negativity constraint was removed for the risk-free asset, would borrow money endlessly for investing in portfolio *OR*. Such behaviour seems to contradict Roy's claim that unfavourable outcomes should be avoided as best as possible, and is certainly contradicted by observation.

Telser's (1955/56) critique of Roy's decision rule also aims at the missing risk-free asset. He points out that Roy's safety first principle might lead to choosing a portfolio with a negative expected return.[65] Telser is wrong in stating that the investors then 'could expect to lose money on their portfolio',[66] since 'expected value' and 'outcome to expect' are not equivalent. But he is right in claiming that Roy's rule implies that there is no asset that the investor can hold without risk. He argues that, in the short run, money can be considered a risk-free asset, yielding $r_f = 0$. Telser claims that in this case an investor should prefer not investing at all to investing in a portfolio with a negative expected value.

His argument is thus that Roy's decision situation does not cover all possible portfolio choice situations. Telser first separates all possible

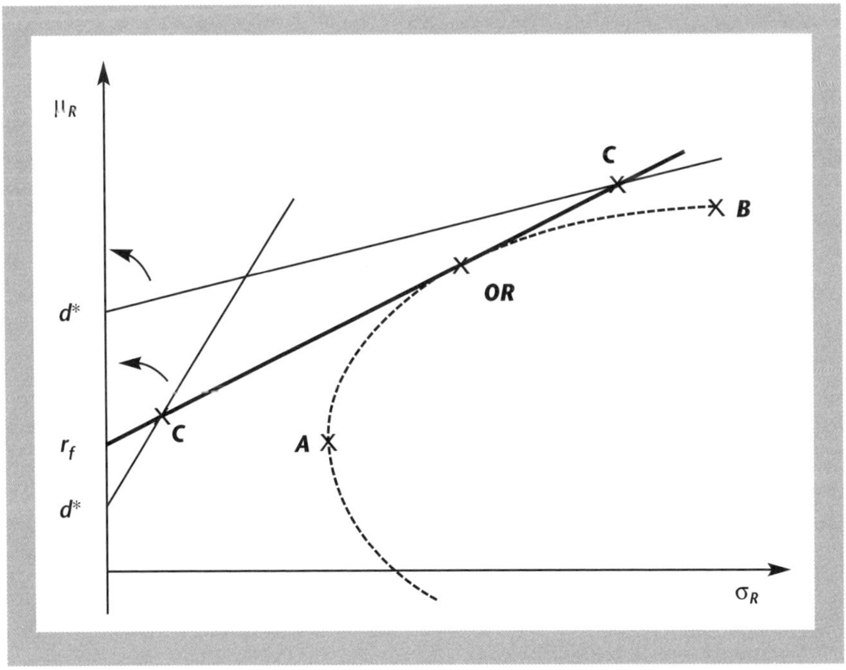

Figure 3.4 Portfolio choice in Roy's model with a risk-free asset

portfolios into two classes. The first class consists of all investments having $P(R = r \leq d^*) \leq \alpha$, which he calls the 'admissible class'. The second class equivalently consists of all investments having $P(R = r \leq d^*) > \alpha$. α is thus the level of probability that must not be exceeded. Among the admissible class the portfolio with the highest expected value is chosen. Telser's safety first rule thus assigns a preference index to all gambles according to

$$\Psi(G) = \psi(\mu_R, 0) = \begin{cases} E[R] & \text{if } P(R = r \leq d^*) \leq \alpha \\ 0 & \text{if } P(R = r \leq d^*) > \alpha \end{cases}$$

Any subjective evaluation of the returns is missing again, but this can again be remedied by exchanging utilities for returns, or by assuming $u(r) = r$. No normative considerations on rationality can serve to accept or reject Telser's rule.

It may, however, be criticised on two counts, which will again be demonstrated graphically. With the help of Chebyshev's inequality,

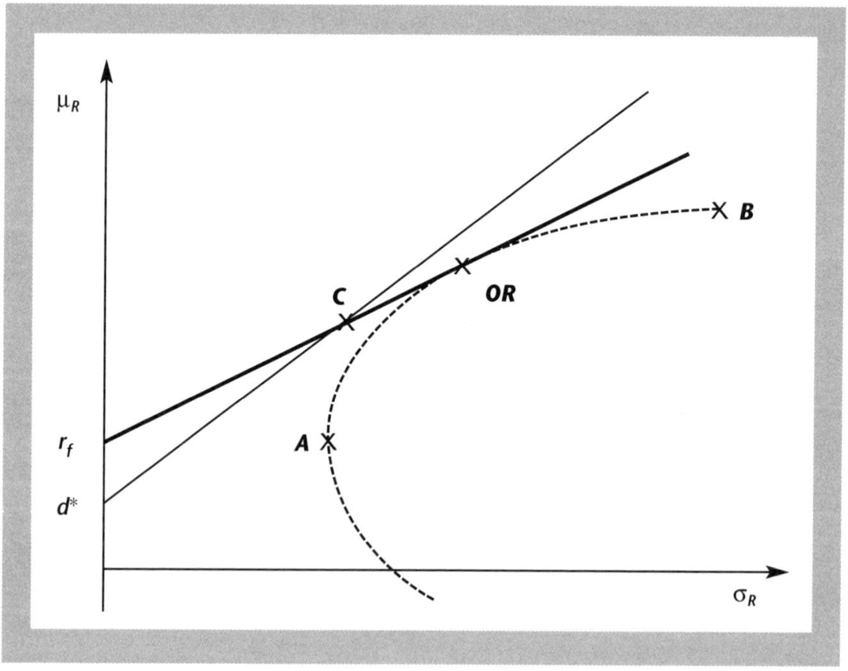

Figure 3.5 Portfolio choice in Telser's model

Telser's decision rule can also be separated into the same two steps as above. The first step yields the efficient set as depicted in Figure 3.5. Since both α and d^* are given, the most preferred portfolio of this efficient set may be found graphically by drawing a line of positive slope from the point $(0, d^*)$. The slope is determined by the probability α. The lower α, the steeper the slope. Since the 'admissible class' is given by $P(R = r \leq d^*) \leq \alpha$, the area above this line holds all admissible portfolios. If $d^* < r_f$, the most preferred portfolio is found where the line starting in $(0, d^*)$ intersects the efficient set. All portfolios on this line are a combination of the risk-free asset and the optimal risky portfolio *OR*. Thus, Telser's safety first rule recommends and explains diversification behaviour in case a risk-free asset exists. Furthermore, the lower α, that is, the lower the accepted probability of disaster, the more money is held, which is reasonable.

On the other hand, Telser's rule has limited applicability in case $d^* > r_f$. If the probability of disaster α is set such that the slope of the line separating the admissible class of portfolios from the inadmissible class is steeper than the slope of the efficient set, no intersection and no solution exist. This case is illustrated in Figure 3.6.

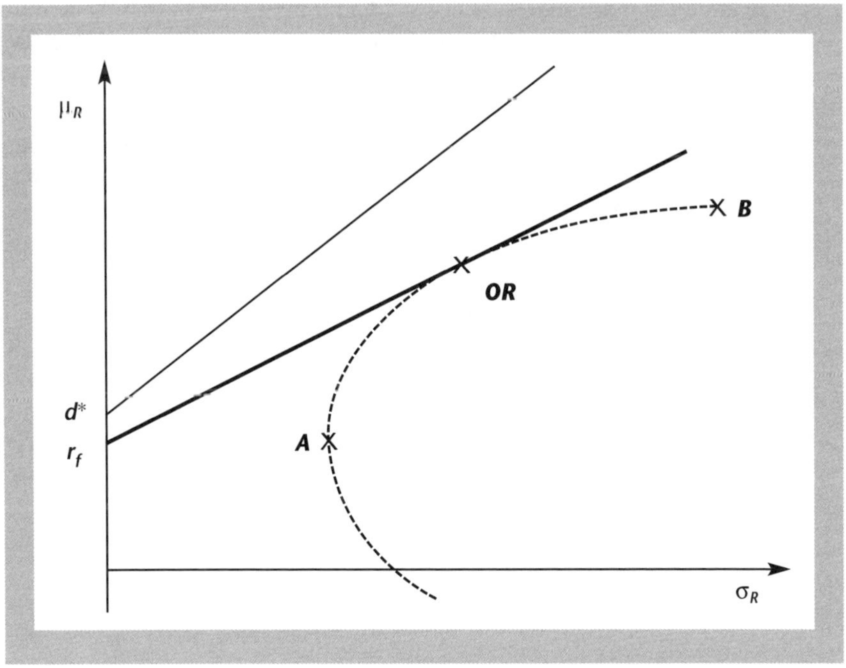

Figure 3.6 Portfolio choice in Telser's model with $d^* > r_f$

Thus, situations may be constructed to which Telser's safety first rule is inapplicable. This is a consequence of the missing possibility to trade the disaster level d^*, or the probability of disaster α, against a measure of return, like the expected value. Telser himself mentions this shortcoming, but deliberately sets both d^* and α fixed to keep the analysis simple.[67]

In contrast, Markowitz's rule includes such a trade-off between the 'risk' and the 'return to expect', which is one of its advantages. His recommendation is to weigh the advantages of a portfolio, measured by the expected value, against the disadvantages, measured by the variance. If no risk-free asset exists, the most preferred portfolio according to Markowitz's rule will be an element of the efficient set of risky portfolios. If a risk-free asset exists, the most preferred portfolio will be a linear combination of the risk-free asset and the risky portfolio *OR*. The weights attributed to the risk-free asset and the risk-bearing portfolio depend on the specific decision rule. Thus, Markowitz's decision rule is applicable more generally than either Roy's or Telser's.

Further criticism may be levelled against Telser's choice of the expected value for the risk preference function. As has been argued, the expected value finds support in the law of large numbers. Its assertion is based on infinitely many repeats, whereas Telser, like Roy, refers to single-period investments. This is evident from his separating the admissible from the inadmissible portfolios by their probability of disaster. Employing the expected value stands in direct contradiction to his intention. Therefore, there is an inherent contradiction in his decision rule. Decisions are made according to a parameter that is explicitly or implicitly linked to infinitely many repeats, whereas the entire decision situation, the notion of risk, and the claimed intention, is based on a single period. There is mismatching between the parameters of the decision rule with the situations to which it is applied.

Kataoka (1963) shares the concern towards choosing the expected value as the main decision criterion. Without further explanation, he states that 'the expected value [...] is not always considered a good measure for the optimality criterion'.[68] Instead of maximising the expected value, he suggests choosing the portfolio with the highest α-percentage-point, or α-quantile, denoted ξ_α, where α is the fixed probability of the investment resulting in an outcome lower than ξ_α. His rule thus assigns a preference index to every gamble by

$$\Psi(G) = \psi(\xi_\alpha) = \xi_\alpha$$

with $P(R = r \leq \xi_\alpha) = \alpha$. This probability is sometimes considered a conditional equation of Kataoka's decision rule, which it is not. It is simply the definition of the α-quantile for continuous distributions. For discrete distributions, the definition is $P(R = r \leq \xi_\alpha) \leq \alpha$, because discrete distributions may not have an exact α-quantile. This latter definition is prone to misinterpretations. It is not required, or possible, to both maximise ξ_α, and minimise α, as $P(R = r \leq \xi_\alpha) \leq \alpha$ might make one believe. The probability α must be chosen in advance and ξ_α is the variate's α-value whose cumulative probability is closest to it, without exceeding it. The preference index simply postulates choosing the gamble with the highest α-quantile.

Kataoka's decision rule is quite intuitive. Between gambles with equal dispersion it leads to choosing the one whose probability distribution lies furthest to the right, as measured by its probability mass. It is similar to Wald's rule,[69] which is applicable to situations under Knightian uncertainty. Wald's rule suggests choosing the action with the highest minimum utility possible, that is,

$$G_i \succeq G_k \quad \text{if} \quad \min_j u_{i,j} \geq \min_j u_{i,k}$$

for discrete random variables. Kataoka, referring to continuous random variables, substitutes the α-percentage point ξ_α for the minimum possible utility. Both may thus be considered maximin rules.

Graphically, Kataoka's rule may be explained using the same setting as above. It is depicted in Figure 3.7. Since the probability α is given, maximising ξ_α is equivalent to a parallel shift of a ray, the slope of which is equivalent to the probability α, starting from an arbitrary point on the ordinate. This ray is denoted d' in Figure 3.7. If no risk-free asset is assumed to exist, the optimal portfolio is found where this ray is a tangent to the efficient set of risky portfolios. The choice made is again denoted as portfolio C.

It is, however, not implausible to assume that a risk-free asset exists, because Kataoka refers to single investments. If a risk-free asset is assumed to exist, his safety first rule may fail to explain observable diversification behaviour. If $P(R = r \leq \xi_a) = \alpha$ is such that the slope of the ray separating admissible from inadmissible investments is steeper than the slope of the tangent from point $(0, r_f)$ to the efficient set, Kataoka's decision rule recommends investing everything in the risk-free asset.[70] If

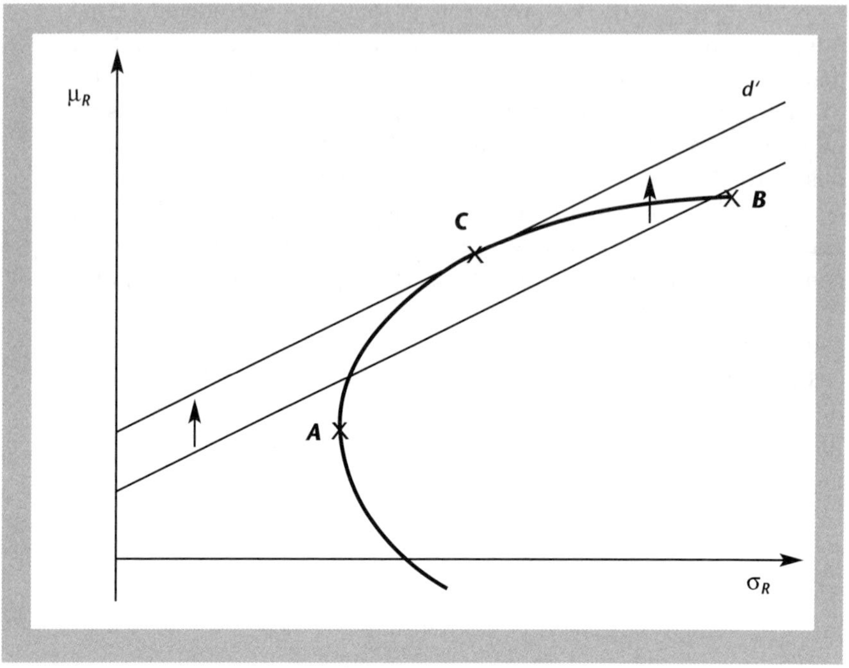

Figure 3.7 Portfolio choice in Kataoka's model

$P(R = r \leq \xi_a) = \alpha$ is such that the slope of the ray separating admissible from inadmissible investments is flatter than the slope of the tangent from point (0, r_f) to the efficient set, Kataoka's decision rule still recommends investing everything in portfolio *C*. This case is illustrated in Figure 3.8.

If the non-negativity constraint for the risk-free asset is dropped, Kataoka's decision rule recommends borrowing endlessly and investing all that is borrowed in portfolio *OR*. Obviously, in cases where a risk-free return is available, the decision rule can only recommend either/or. No in-between can be recommended. No division of investable wealth between the risk-free asset and portfolio *OR* is quantifiable.

It must thus again be concluded that decision rules that do not allow for any trade-off between two or more characteristics of the portfolios' distributions may in some conceivable decision situations fail to recommend or explain diversification behaviour. It is no surprise then that Markowitz's rule, being applicable more generally than the rules of Roy, Telser and Kataoka, received prime attention in portfolio choice theory. It

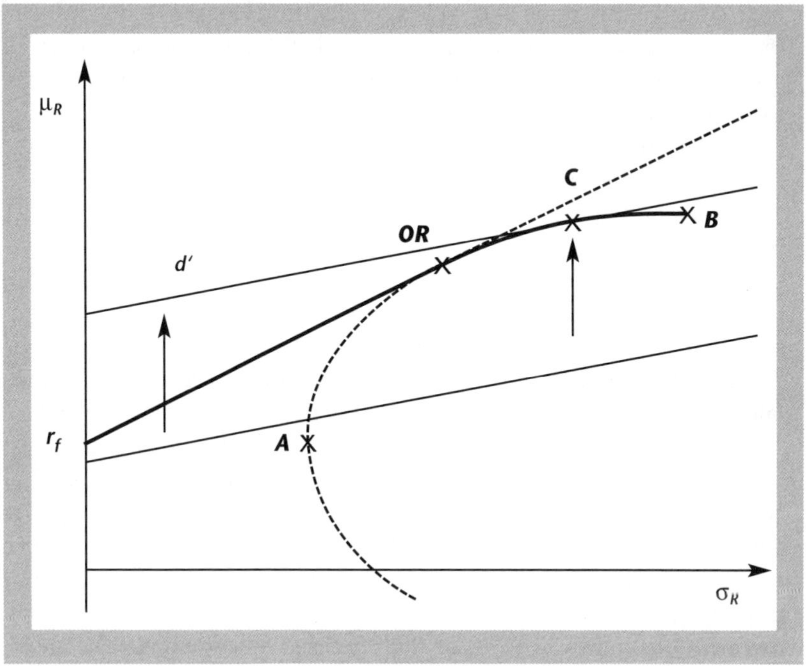

Figure 3.8 Portfolio choice in Kataoka's model with a risk-free asset

is only due to criticism brought against the descriptive validity of the variance as a measure of the 'risk' of an investment that the ideas behind the safety first rules regained some ground in more recent contributions.

3.6 MORE RECENT CONTRIBUTIONS

Most decision rules proposed as alternatives to Markowitz's μ–σ^2 rule should be regarded as amendments to his rule, rather than true alternatives. They focus on single aspects. These aspects are first declared implausible or inadequate according to some standard.

The first kind of criticism is levelled against the μ–σ^2 rule's lack of congruence with the EU principle, thus declaring the EU principle's definition of rationality the standard against which all decision rules have to be measured. This kind of criticism was sparked by Markowitz himself, who accepted the EU principle as the standard for 'rationality'. Proponents of the EU principle will insist that Markowitz's μ–σ^2 rule can only be 'rational' either if the μ–σ^2 rule's 'utility' function $\varphi(r)$ is quadratic in the returns, or if the returns are normally distributed. The plausibility of assuming quadratic utility functions or normally distributed returns may then be examined. If refuted, alternatives may be proposed. Decision rules emanating from this first kind of criticism will be discussed in the first part of this section.

The second kind of criticism is levelled against the descriptive validity of the variance as a measure of the 'risk' an investor might perceive. Decision rules emanating from this kind of criticism will be discussed in the second part of this section. It is interesting that all decision rules stemming from this second kind of criticism are also claimed to submit to the EU principle's definition of rationality. All proposed amendments thus fall under the criticism levelled against the EU principle in section 3.3.

For the purpose of this treatise, their analysis would thus be unnecessary. This is also true for decision rules stemming from the first kind of criticism when they are merely special cases of the EU principle. A detailed analysis is conducted nevertheless, not least because any treatise on decision rules for portfolio choice would be incomplete without discussing the more recent contributions. In addition, the analysis will reveal shortcomings of some of the proposed amendments. The shortcomings range from violating the self-imposed EU standard of 'rationality' up to failing to meet their set objectives.

Starting with the first kind of criticism, it has been shown in section 3.4 that the risk attitude function of Markowitz's μ–σ^2 rule has to be quadratic in the returns, if the EU principle is to be obeyed. Markowitz's rule is then also quadratic in money wealth, since returns and terminal wealth are by definition connected as $W_T = w_0(1 + R_T)$, where W_T is the wealth at the end of period T, and w_0 is initial wealth. Although 'rational' by the EU principle's standards, quadratic risk attitude functions have been labelled 'implausible', because they imply increasing 'absolute risk aversion'. Absolute risk aversion is defined as the negative ratio of the 'utility' function's second and first derivative, that is, $A(w_T) = [-\omega''(w_T)/\omega'(w_T)]$.[71] Arrow (1971) argues that this measure should decrease with increasing initial wealth. This is also suggested by Blume and Friend (1975), and Friend and Blume (1975). This kind of criticism leads to a rejection of Markowitz's quadratic 'utility' function, because it displays increasing absolute risk aversion.

Several other 'utility' functions are proposed instead, like exponential, logarithmic and power functions.[72] All of these amendments simply argue that portfolio choice decisions should not be made according to Markowitz's rule, but according to some specific EU rule.

Since the EU principle has already been dealt with and its suitability for single period investments questioned, these rules need not be discussed any further here.

Markowitz's μ–σ^2 rule also complies with the EU principle if returns are assumed to be normally distributed. The assumption of normally distributed returns is at times justified by having recourse to the central limit theorem.[73] If an investment horizon T is divided into τ investment periods, $t = 1,..., \tau$, the return of a single asset or a portfolio over the period T may be expressed as

$$(1+R_T) = (1+R_1)(1+R_2)(1+R_3)...(1+R_\tau)$$

Taking natural logarithms yields

$$\ln(1+R_T) = \ln(1+R_1) + \ln(1+R_2) + \ln(1+R_3) +...+ \ln(1+R_\tau)$$

Then, if period returns are assumed to be independent and identically distributed, the central limit theorem applies. It states that $\ln(1+R_T)$ is normally distributed for $\tau \to \infty$. Since an approximation procedure is associated with the central limit theorem, it is claimed that the limiting distribution may be used even if τ is finite. Furthermore, since $\ln(1+R_t) \approx R_t$ if R_t lies, roughly, between -0.15 and $+0.15$, it is also claimed that the R_t may be assumed to be normally distributed.

Thus, if the expected value and the variance of the random variables $\ln(1+R_t)$ exist, the central limit theorem is taken as justification for assuming normally distributed returns. Even if the $\ln(1+R_t)$ have no finite variances, there still exists a sufficient condition for the central limit theorem to be applicable. It suffices that the $\ln(1+R_t)$ are independent and uniformly bounded by some value h, and that $V[\ln(1+R_T)] \to \infty$ for $\tau \to \infty$. In this case, $\ln(1+R_T)$ is also normally distributed for $\tau \to \infty$.[74] This sufficient condition may support claims that a μ–σ^2 rule is approximately applicable if the returns' distributions have low probability of 'extreme' values. Such a claim is made by Levy and Markowitz (1979) and Kroll et al. (1984).

But there is a serious objection against justifying the normality assumption with the central limit theorem. Applying the standard theorems for the expected value and the variance of a sum of independent, identically distributed random variables to $\ln(1+R_T)$ yields $E[\ln(1+R_T)] = \tau \cdot E[\ln(1+R_t)]$ and $V[\ln(1+R_T)] = \tau \cdot V[\ln(1+R_t)]$. The expected value and variance of $\ln(1+R_T)$ are thus not finite for $\tau \to \infty$, and the infinite expected value and variance obviously render the μ–σ^2 rule inapplicable. Although it is true that a sum of independent variates has a normal limiting distribution, this limiting distribution is degenerate. The central limit theorem is only useful for standardised variates, which have as their limiting distribution the standard normal distribution.

Of course, as long as τ is finite, the expected value and the variance of $\ln(1+R_T)$ will also be finite, providing the expected value and the variance of $\ln(1+R_t)$ are finite, and the normal distribution may serve as an approximation. But such approximations necessitate the introduction of thresholds of discernment, which violate Debreu's axioms, and any violation of Debreu's axioms prohibits the use of decision rules to indicate preference relations. The assumption of normally distributed returns must thus be made outright. It cannot be justified by the central limit theorem in the context of portfolio decisions.

It comes as no surprise that the outright assumption of normally distributed returns has also been questioned. Empirical investigations conducted by Mandelbrot (1963) and Fama (1965a), among others,[75] lead them to claim that a non-normal stable Paretian distribution fits return data better than a normal distribution. Stable Paretian distributions are classified as being invariant under addition. More precisely, let $X_1, X_2, X_3, \ldots, X_n$ denote mutually independent random variables with a common distribution D, and let $S_n = X_1 + X_2 + X_3 + \ldots + X_n$. The distribution D is called stable Paretian, if for all n there exist constants $c_n > 0$ and d_n such that S_n has the same distribution as $c_nX + d_n$.[76]

Stable distributions are members of a four-parameter family of distributions. The parameters are commonly denoted by α to δ. α, bounded by $0 < \alpha \leq 2$, is known as the characteristic exponent. Together with β, which is bounded by $-1 \leq \beta \leq 1$, α determines the 'type' of the distribution. For $\alpha = 2$, the random variable has a normal distribution; for $\alpha = 1$, which induces $\beta = 0$, the random variable has a Cauchy distribution. The characteristic exponent α also determines the total probability contained in the distribution's peak and tails. If $\alpha < 2$, the distribution is 'leptokurtic', meaning that its tails contain more probability mass than the tails of the normal distribution. The most important characteristic of a stable Paretian distribution with $\alpha < 2$ is that it does not have a finite variance. The variance is finite only if $\alpha = 2$, that is, the normal distribution is the only stable Paretian distribution with a finite variance. If returns follow a stable Paretian distribution with parameter $\alpha < 2$, Markowitz's μ–σ^2 rule is thus not only 'irrational'. It becomes inapplicable altogether. Not even the central limit theorem can be applied, since the distribution is also unbounded. Fama concludes, 'the Markowitz definition of an efficient portfolio loses its meaning'[77] in a world of stable Paretian distributions with $\alpha < 2$.

As an amendment, Fama suggests using the parameter γ as an alternative measure for the distribution's dispersion. Together, the parameters β, γ and δ determine the distribution's skewness, scale and location. Unfortunately, γ is a parameter of the characteristic function, not of the density function. Only in two special cases does γ correspond to a parameter of the density function. The first case is the Cauchy case, having $\alpha = 1$ and $\beta = 0$. Here γ is equal to the 'semi-interquartile range', that is, to half the distance between the first and the third quartile. But the Cauchy distribution does not have a finite expected value. Paretian distributions have finite expected values only if $\alpha > 1$. The expected value is then equal to the parameter δ. In the Cauchy case, the expected value is infinite and the parameter δ is equal to the median or modal value. Since Fama proposes using the expected value, the Cauchy distribution is of no use.

The other special case where γ corresponds to a parameter of the density function is the Gaussian case. In this case $\alpha = 2$ and γ is equal to $\sigma^2/2$. But then Markowitz's μ–σ^2 rule is applicable and 'rational', and the criticism levelled against it unjustified. In all other cases, a computational definition of the parameter γ is not available. Fama suggests approximating the parameter γ by the intersextile range of the distribution.[78] If this suggestion is cast into a decision rule, Fama's analysis may be translated into proposing a rule that assigns a preference index to all gambles according to

$$\Psi(G) = \psi\left(\mu_R, \xi_{1-1/6} - \xi_{1/6}\right)$$ [79]

A very similar decision rule seems to have been thought of by Lange (1944), who implicitly recommends using the median together with the distribution's range in the case of discrete distributions, or the median together with the distribution's interquartile range in the case of continuous distributions.[80]

Whether Fama's decision rule withstands empirical observation on investors' behaviour has not been tested. Normative considerations on the 'rationality' of the decision rule implied by Fama's analysis would be unnecessary, had Fama not explicitly embedded his analysis within the EU principle's framework.[81] Thus, a few thoughts on the congruence of decision rules that rest on ordinal parameters with the EU principle may be added here.

Schneeweiß (1967) states that a decision rule comprising the expected value and some ordinal parameters is consistent with the EU principle if and only if (1) it is a function of the expected value alone and (2) if the EU principle's risk attitude function is linear.[82] Schneeweiß then concludes that any decision rule employing the expected value together with percentiles is 'irrational' by the EU principle's standards. Thus, Fama's decision rule faces a dilemma. Normally distributed returns ensure that Markowitz's μ–σ^2 rule is 'rational' in the EU principle's sense, but Fama questions the normality assumption. Replacing the normality assumption by assuming that returns follow a stable Paretian distribution renders Markowitz's μ–σ^2 rule inapplicable. But Fama arrives at a decision rule that must be considered 'irrational' by the EU principle's standard itself. Fama succeeds in deducting diversification effects in a stable Paretian framework, and also in deriving an efficient set. But he fails to submit the analysis under the EU principle's maxim. This causes an air of incompleteness and contradiction, and renders his proposal unattractive.

Further empirical studies led to the conclusion, first, that frequency distributions of returns may alternatively be explained by the Student-t-distribution,[83] or by a mixture of normal distributions,[84] and, second, that the stability property of the stable Paretian hypothesis cannot be observed empirically for returns of different periods.[85] In the end, the normal hypothesis is accepted, at least for monthly returns, on evidence provided by Blattberg and Gonedes (1974), and later by Fama (1976) himself.

The first kind of criticism levelled against Markowitz's μ–σ^2 rule, the stated lack of congruence with the EU principle, has thus not led to any genuine contribution. Either some special EU rule is proposed instead, or rules are designed that do not comply with the EU definition of rationality either. In this treatise, compliance with the EU principle is not considered a necessary or sufficient criterion for normative decision rules. The objection raised here is that the common feature of all the above proposals, their reliance on expected values, makes them seek implicit support from the law of large numbers. But the law of large numbers is applicable only to situations of infinitely many repeats.

Turning to the second kind of criticism levelled against Markowitz's μ–σ^2 rule, it can be said that it is of an entirely different nature. It questions the variance's validity as a descriptive measure for the 'risk' an investor might feel confronted with. The intuitive appeal of Markowitz's decision rule, based on a dichotomy into 'risk' and 'return', caused a digression of the term 'risk' from its original meaning. Being in fact a characteristic of a specific decision situation, it is often considered an autonomous quantity.

The parameter used to measure the 'risk' involved in a decision situation is then considered liable to descriptive validity. It is claimed that the variance cannot describe 'risk' properly, since it includes both negative and positive deviations from the expected value. 'Risk', it is argued over and over again, should only be associated with negative deviations from a certain 'target' return. This view, which is reminiscent of the view expressed in the safety first rules discussed in section 3.5, has today become the main driving force behind portfolio choice theory.

The arguments are typically not of a truly descriptive nature. No empirical investigations into observable decision behaviour are conducted. The proposed risk measures are based on intuitive reasoning, on introspection, and on claims that 'decision makers in investment contexts very frequently associate risk with failure to attain a target return'.[86] All developments that are based on this kind of argument are appropriately referred to as 'downside risk approaches'.

This now predominant field of portfolio choice theory was initiated by Markowitz (1959) himself, who might have anticipated this kind of criticism against the variance. Unfortunately, all contributions stemming from this field suffer from a severe blurring of the distinction between normative and descriptive theory. Although designed to overcome a suspected descriptive shortcoming, and although thus by definition descriptive decision rules, all 'downside risk' approaches try to gather further support by submitting themselves to the EU principle's definition of 'rationality'. This kind of reliance on the EU principle's notion of 'rationality' is, of course, an undue mixture of descriptive and normative reasoning. The unfortunate blurring of these two perspectives has already been noted for many developments in the field of general EU theory, but it is particularly apparent in recent contributions to portfolio choice theory.

It seems that Markowitz has exerted another overwhelming influence here. He introduces his μ–σ^2 rule both as a normative and as a descriptive rule,[87] thus inviting criticism from both sides. This may have contributed to the lack of distinction between the two perspectives, which has culminated in claims that 'adequate', or 'correct', or 'optimal' risk measures should be discussed without any regard to decision theory in general, or to risk preference functions and decision rules in particular.[88]

This view is not shared here, as has been stated in Chapter 2. The 'downside risk' approaches will be discussed within a decision theory framework. Their hybrid form allows them to be analysed either from a normative or from a descriptive point of view. As descriptive rules, they should be put under the scrutiny of empirical testing. This will not be done here, since the following chapters will focus on proposing normative decision rules. Suffice it to note that like any other decision rule, 'downside risk' rules must rely on Debreu's axioms. But Debreu's axioms have been falsified empirically.

As normative rules, they are irrefutable, unless they try to gather additional support by submitting themselves to the EU principle and thus implicitly by relying on the law of large numbers. Then they are recommendable only for situations of infinitely many repeats. Since this argument has been given repeatedly, any further analysis is unnecessary.

Although not fitting neatly into the general topic of this treatise, a close examination of 'downside risk' approaches will nevertheless be conducted here. Downside risk approaches have found widespread approval, and their prominence justifies a special if separate treatment. The result of the analysis also justifies it being included here. It will become apparent that most proposed 'downside risk' approaches fail to meet the EU principle's criteria for 'rationality', while some even fail to achieve their own objective.

When analysing the μ–σ^2 rule's compliance with the EU principle, Markowitz lists five alternative 'measures of risk'.[89] These measures are the expected absolute deviation, the maximum loss, the expected value of loss, the probability of loss and the semi-variance. The exact definitions of these quantities will be given below. All of them, except the expected absolute deviation, may be considered 'downside risk measures'.

With this list Markowitz sets the standard for all subsequent 'downside risk' analysis. First, because all further 'downside risk' contributions focus on these quantities, albeit defining them more generally at times. Second, 'rationality' remains firmly embedded within the EU principle's framework. Markowitz calls the EU principle 'reasonable offhand' and believes 'that the arguments in favour of the expected utility maxim are quite convincing, especially for its application in areas such as portfolio selection'.[90] He judges the 'rationality' of a decision principle not only by its compliance with the EU principle, but also by the 'plausibility' of the 'utility' function's mathematical form that the EU principle imposes on them.

This argument is similar in kind to the one described at the beginning of this chapter. As mentioned there, some proponents of the EU principle criticise Markowitz's rule for displaying 'absolute risk aversion', that is, for the shape of the 'utility' function that the EU principle imposes on them. The proposals described now are also judged by the shape of their imposed 'utility' function, although the criticism now stems from the alleged lack of descriptive validity. For example, Schneeweiß (1967) bases his rejection of the probability of loss and the semi-variance on the lack of 'plausibility' of their 'utility' function.

The first three alternative risk measures listed by Markowitz, the expected absolute deviation, the maximum loss and the expected value of loss, need not be discussed in great detail. If they can be made to comply with the EU principle, they imply 'utility' functions that are deemed implausible by the EU principle's proponents. They have thus not received much further attention.

The expected absolute deviation from a target return d may be generally defined as $E\left[\left|r-b\right|\right]$. It is the only non-'downside risk' measure on Markowitz's list. Combined with the expected value it implies a 'utility' function consisting of two linear segments that meet at $r=d$. Markowitz considers such a risk attitude function 'objectionable'.

The maximum loss is rejected as a measure of risk because no decision rule comprising expected value and maximum loss complies with the EU principle. As can easily be verified, such a decision rule violates the independence axiom.

The expected value of loss was first proposed by Domar and Musgrave (1944). The term 'expected value of loss' is misleading. The quantity should rather be called the 'probability or density weighted sum of left-hand deviations from zero'. A more general quantity, substituting $r=0$ by some target return d, may also be used. No matter what version is used, proponents of the EU principle reject decision rules consisting of the expected value and this risk measure because of the shape of the 'utility' function needed to make it comply with the EU principle. The EU principle imposes a function that consists of two linear segments of different slopes meeting at $r=0$ or $r=d$.

The more interesting alternatives that Markowitz lists are the probability of loss and the semi-variance. Decision rules comprising the expected value and the probability of loss, or, more generally, the probability of sustaining a return below some pre-specified target return d, have been discussed by Allais (1953), Albach (1962), Pruitt (1962) and Schneeweiß (1967), among others. These decision rules assign a preference index to all gambles according to

$$\Psi(G)=\psi(\mu,F(d))$$

with $F(d)$ denoting the cumulative probability $P(R = r < d)$. Here, the ideas of Roy, Telser and Kataoka are obviously embedded. But although this decision rule is reminiscent of safety first rules, it is of a different nature. The rule provides for a trade-off between μ and $F(d)$, whereas safety first rules do not, as discussed in section 3.5. When confronted with the EU maxim, the function $\psi(\mu, F(d))$ does have to be linear and the decision rule then consists of two parallel linear segments separated by a discontinuity at $r = d$.[91] Schneeweiß, a proponent of the EU principle, has thus rejected this decision rule as 'rational, but not very sensible'.[92]

The so-called 'semi-variance' has received the greatest attention and today is firmly established within portfolio choice theory. It may generally be defined as the weighted squared deviations of the returns from a target return d, that is,

$$SV_d = \int_{-\infty}^{\infty} (d - r)^2 \, dF(r)$$

The popularity of this 'risk measure' is again based solely on its intuitive appeal, not on any normative reasoning or alternative definitions of rationality. Markowitz claims that 'analyses based on S[emi-variance] tend to produce better portfolios than those based on V[ariance]', simply because an analysis based on semi-variance 'concentrates on reducing losses'.[93] He also claims that 'semi-variance is the more plausible measure of risk'.[94] This kind of intuitive reasoning has been adopted by many authors.[95] Decision rules employing μ and SV_d have also been discussed by Mao (1970a, b), Hogan and Warren (1972, 1974), Porter (1974), Bawa (1975), Fishburn (1977) and others.

The semi-variance is a special case of a more general 'risk measure', the so-called 'lower partial moment of order n'. Lower partial moments (LPM) of order n, introduced by Bawa (1976, 1978) and Fishburn (1977), are defined as

$$LPM_d^n = \int_{-\infty}^{d} (d - r)^n \, \mathrm{d}F(r)$$

For $n = 0$, the lower partial moment is equivalent to the probability of loss. Setting $n = 1$ yields the density weighted sum of left-hand deviations from the value d. The lower partial moment of order $n = 2$ is equivalent to the semi-variance.[96] Fishburn justifies using lower partial moments of a higher order than $n = 2$ by simply claiming that there is 'no compelling a priori reason' for not using them.[97]

Again, the terms 'semi-variance' and 'lower partial moment' are misleading, since only a part of the probability or density function of R is used for calculating them. They are not moments of the distribution of the random variable R, but moments of a transformed mixed distribution, which concentrates the probability mass of the density function left to d on this value. Sometimes the terms 'target-semivariance'[98] and 'target lower partial moments' are used to distinguish the versions using a general target from the version using $d = 0$ as the target.[99] But μ–SV_d decision rules and μ–LPM_d^n decision rules with $d \neq E[R]$ comply with the EU principle only if the 'utility' function $\omega(r)$, or for $u(r) = r$ the risk attitude function $\varphi(r)$, is given by

$$\varphi(u(r)) = \varphi(r) = \begin{cases} r - k(d - r)^n & \text{if} \quad r < d \\ r & \text{if} \quad r \geq d \end{cases}$$

with k a positive constant.[100] The implied risk attitude function $\varphi(r)$ again consists of two segments. The segment for returns above d is a straight line and thus displays constant absolute risk aversion. The segment associated with returns below d is a straight line for $n = 0$ and $n = 1$. For $n = 2$, the segment associated with returns below d is quadratic, as is the equivalent segment of Markowitz's rule.

Thus, when the μ–σ^2 rule is rejected because its risk attitude function displays increasing absolute risk aversion, μ–SV_d rules and μ–LPM_d^n rules must be rejected as well. The same is true for all other lower partial moments. For all $n \geq 3$, the segment associated with returns below the 'target return' d displays increasing absolute risk aversion. This can easily be verified by calculating the appropriate derivatives and applying them to the Pratt–Arrow measure of risk aversion. The fact that these rules display risk attitude functions that have been labelled 'implausible' in connection with the μ–σ^2 rule must be considered a severe shortcoming. The critique levelled against Markowitz's rule in the first place simply carries over in part to some of the alternatives proposed.

In spite of this severe shortcoming, μ–LPM_d^n rules have received widespread attention and approval. This is not simply due to their intuitive appeal. It is foremost due to some now prominent and often cited contributions by Bawa (1975, 1978), Fishburn (1977), Bawa and Lindenberg (1977), Harlow and Rao (1988) and Harlow (1991). These contributions seemingly reconcile decision rules that comprise expected values and some lower partial moments with the EU principle and 'plausible' risk attitude. It will prove illuminating to discuss this pseudo-reconciliation.

Bawa (1975, 1978) and Fishburn (1977) justify the use of lower partial moments in classical decision rules by having recourse to 'stochastic dominance rules'. Stochastic dominance rules postulate preferring a gamble G_1 to a gamble G_2, if G_1 'stochastically dominates' G_2. Three kinds of stochastic dominance are commonly distinguished, referred to as stochastic dominance of orders one, two and three. For situations of Knightian risk if $r_i > r_j$ implies that $r_i \succ r_j$,[101] stochastic dominance of first order may be stated as follows: if $F_1(r) \leq F_2(r)\ \forall\ r$, where $F_1(r)$ and $F_2(r)$ are the cumulative distribution functions of the gambles G_1 and G_2, then G_1 stochastically dominates G_2.[102]

As a decision rule, stochastic dominance of order one thus simply postulates that G_1 is preferred to G_2, if for any given result r^* $P(R = r \leq r^*)$ is for G_1 lower than for G_2. Graphically, a gamble G_1 is preferred to a gamble G_2, if and only if its cumulative distribution function never lies above and somewhere below that of G_2.[103] As a decision rule, second-order stochastic dominance postulates that a gamble G_1 is preferred to a gamble G_2, if and only if the integral of its cumulative distribution function never lies above and somewhere below that of G_2.[104] The third-order stochastic dominance rule postulates that a gamble G_1 is preferred to a gamble G_2, if its expected value is higher or equal to that of G_2, and if the integral's integral of its cumulative distribution function never lies above and somewhere below that of G_2.[105]

The appealing feature of stochastic dominance rules is that they identify the same sets of gambles that the EU principle identifies under certain restrictions on the risk attitude function $\varphi(u)$.[106] Stochastic dominance rules thus not only submit themselves to the EU principle's definition of rationality, they also submit themselves to restrictions on the risk attitude function that, according to Bawa, 'follow from prevalent and appealing modes of economic behaviour'.[107] The restrictions are those introduced by Arrow, Pratt and Blume and Friend, as mentioned at the beginning of this chapter.

Formally, with $\varphi^{(i)}(u)$ denoting the ith derivative of $\varphi(u)$, the restrictions define subclasses of risk attitude functions with the following characteristics:

1. $\varphi_1(u) = \{\ \varphi(u)\ \big|\ \varphi^{(1)}(u) > 0\ , \qquad \forall\ u \in \mathbf{U}\}$
2. $\varphi_2(u) = \{\ \varphi(u)\ \big|\ \varphi^{(1)}(u) > 0 \wedge \varphi^{(2)}(u) < 0\ , \qquad \forall\ u \in \mathbf{U}\}$
3. $\varphi_3(u) = \{\ \varphi(u)\ \big|\ \varphi^{(1)}(u) > 0 \wedge \varphi^{(2)}(u) < 0 \wedge \varphi^{(3)}(u) > 0\ , \qquad \forall\ u \in \mathbf{U}\}$

$\varphi_1(u)$ is the class of increasing risk attitude functions, $\varphi_2(u)$ is the class of increasing risk attitude functions with decreasing marginal risk attitude, which defines 'risk aversion' within the EU maxim, and $\varphi_3(u)$ is the class of 'risk averse' risk attitude functions with a 'skewness preference'. A positive third derivative is implied by a Pratt–Arrow measure of absolute risk aversion that decreases with increasing initial wealth.

The recourse to stochastic dominance rules is interesting because of the following results. The first-order stochastic dominance rule identifies exactly that set of preferred gambles that is also identified by the EU principle under the restriction that only risk attitude functions of kind $\varphi_1(u)$ are considered. The second-order stochastic dominance rule identifies exactly that set of preferred gambles that is also identified by the EU principle under the restriction that only risk attitude functions of kind $\varphi_2(u)$ are considered. The third-order stochastic dominance rule is a sufficient condition for identifying that set of preferred gambles that is identified by the EU principle under the restriction that only risk attitude functions of kind $\varphi_3(u)$ are considered.

The recourse to stochastic dominance rules also bears some interest for portfolio choice problems. There is a connection between stochastic dominance rules and decision rules comprising the expected value as the measure for 'return' and some lower partial moments as the measure for 'risk'. This connection is as follows. Under the same restrictions that have been imposed on the stochastic dominance rules of first, second and third order, the respective sets of preferred gambles may also be identified using lower partial moments in a classical decision rule.[108] Bawa derives three theorems, which state that

(A) a gamble G_1 is preferred to a gamble G_2 for all $\varphi_1(u)$ if and only if
$LPM_d^{n=0}(G_1) \leq LPM_d^{n=0}(G_2)\ \forall\ d \in R$ and $<$ for some d.

(B) a gamble G_1 is preferred to a gamble G_2 for all $\varphi_2(u)$ if and only if
$LPM_d^{n=1}(G_1) \leq LPM_d^{n=1}(G_2)\ \forall\ d \in R$ and $<$ for some d.

(C) a gamble G_1 is preferred to a gamble G_2 for all $\varphi_3(u)$ if and only if
$\mu_1 \geq \mu_2$, and
$LPM_d^{n=2}(G_1) \leq LPM_d^{n=2}(G_2)\ \forall\ d \in R$ and $<$ for some d.

Thus, the set of gambles in (A) is identified either by the EU principle under the restriction that only risk attitude functions of kind $\varphi_1(u)$ are admitted, or by the first-order stochastic dominance rule, or by the gambles' probability of sustaining a return below some pre-specified value d. Likewise, the set of gambles in (B) is identified either by the EU principle under the restriction that only risk attitude functions of kind $\varphi_2(u)$ are admitted, or by the second-order stochastic dominance rule, or by the gambles' density-weighted left-hand deviations from the value d. Finally, the set of gambles in (C) is identified either by the EU principle under the restriction that only risk attitude functions of kind $\varphi_3(u)$ are admitted, or by the third-order stochastic dominance rule, or by the gambles' expected value and semi-variance.[109]

At first glance, these results seem to reconcile μ–LPM rules with the EU principle. They have at least sufficed to firmly embed μ–LPM rules within normative portfolio choice theory. After all, the work of Bawa and Fishburn seems to contradict the result stated earlier, namely that the EU paradigm imposes increasing absolute risk aversion on μ–LPM rules.

But in fact, no contradiction is incurred, because no reconciliation of any μ–LPM rules with the EU principle has been provided. Quite clearly, the contributions cited above are not about decision rules at all. Stochastic dominance rules and their μ–LPM equivalents are restricted to defining what has been called above the 'efficient set' of gambles. Bawa (1978) calls this the 'subset of admissible choices' or the 'admissible set'.[110] All developments that make use of stochastic dominance rules can be characterised by their declaring a gamble G_1 preferred to a gamble G_2, if $E[A] \geq E[B]$ and $LPM_d^n(G_1) \leq LPM_d^n(G_2)$, with at least one strict inequality.[111] Obviously, any such rule is not a decision rule, since no choices among the gambles of the admissible set are possible. How much increase in the expected value is needed to compensate for a given increase in LPM_d^n cannot be specified.[112] But decision rules clearly must be able to identify the single preferred gamble among any set. Both Bawa and Fishburn provide no such rule.

As Markowitz's analysis already indicates, and as can easily be verified, any such decision rule cannot comply with the EU principle, while at the same time have a risk attitude function that belongs to one of the above classes. The claimed reconciliation of lower partial moments as 'risk measures' with the call for 'reasonable' risk attitude functions is achieved only by redefining the problem. Rather than designing decision rules that are able to identify the single most preferred portfolio, the discussion of semi-variance and lower partial moments focuses only on the equivalent to Markowitz's 'efficient set', which is merely the first step in identifying the most preferred portfolio. Thus, as with Fama's contribution discussed earlier, there remains an air of incompleteness and contradiction with this mixture of normative and descriptive analysis.

Hogan and Warren (1974), Bawa and Lindenberg (1977) and Harlow and Rao (1988), who provide market equilibrium relations for asset prices, do avoid decision rules as well. Bawa and Lindenberg and Harlow and Rao claim that portfolio selection problems are problems of calculating the 'admissible set'.[113] But in fact, portfolio selection problems are concerned with choosing among the portfolios of this set. Calculating the 'efficient set' is not enough. The above contributions extend the analyses of Bawa and Fishburn by introducing a risk-free asset. That is, they extend the analysis in the same way in which Tobin extends Markowitz's work.

Again, the new 'admissible set' may be constructed graphically by drawing a function tangential to the admissible set of all risky assets that emanates from the point (r_f, 0). The slope and form of this function depend on the order of the chosen *LPM* and the target return. In Figure 3.9, which is drawn in (μ, $LPM^{1/n}$) space, the tangent function is depicted as linear. This is the case when the risk-free rate is equal to the *LPM*'s target return.[114]

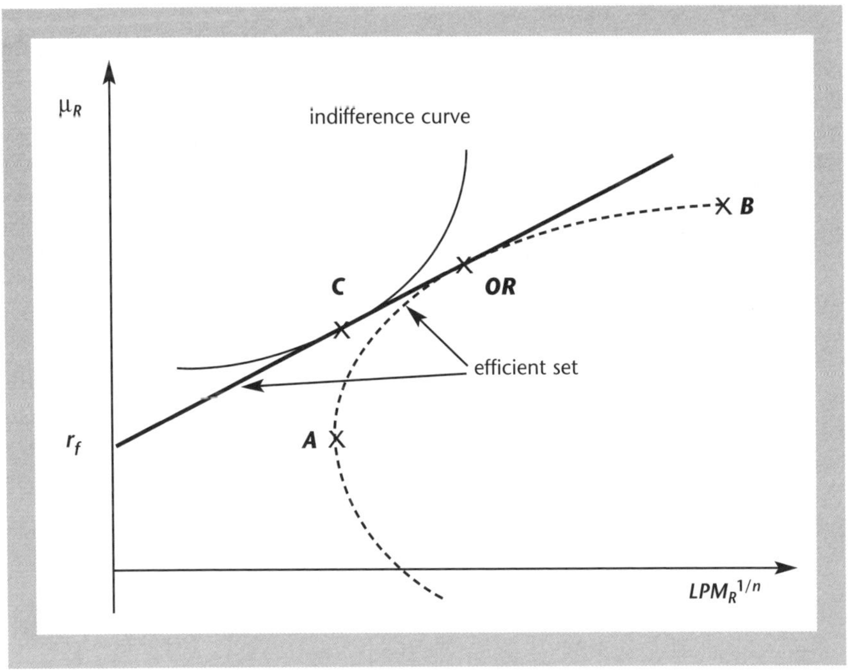

Figure 3.9 Portfolio choice with the μ–*LPM* rule

As is the case with Tobin's extension, and contrary to the above authors' claim, the tangent portfolio, labelled *OR*, is not the most preferred portfolio. It is merely the most preferred 'risky' portfolio. Being able to identify the most preferred 'risky' portfolio does not suffice, of course. This merely translates into determining the weights **x** under exclusion of the risk-free asset. A decision rule must, however, be able to identify the overall preferred portfolio. It must be able to specify the optimal weights of all available assets, including the risk-free asset.

Thus, drawing a line tangential to the admissible set of risky portfolios does not constitute a decision rule if a risk-free asset is included. Identifying portfolio *OR* is not the prime goal. A decision rule has to be able to identify the overall preferred portfolio, labelled *C*. Any such portfolio is again a combination of the optimal risky portfolio and the risk-free asset, if such a risk-free asset exists.

Failure to obtain a decision rule wreaks havoc on any efforts to combine the EU version of rationality with restrictions on the risk attitude function. Additionally, the arguments raised here against the EU principle in general lead to meeting them with reservation even if no restrictions on the risk attitude function are imposed. As it is, most modern analysis contents itself with the intuitive reasoning for choosing 'downside risk' measures.

Holthausen (1981) takes the work of Fishburn (1977) a step further. In his rule, 'risk' is again measured by a probability-weighted function of deviations below a target level. His risk measure is thus the same as proposed by Fishburn, which is a general case of lower partial moments. But the 'return measure' he proposes is not simply the expected value of all returns. It is a mirror image of the risk measure. In Holthausen's rule, 'return' is measured by a probability-weighted function of deviations above some target level. He thus avoids the expected value of the random variable *R*, albeit at the price of using two density-weighted quantities, which are expected values of transformed distributions. The quantities used to measure 'risk' and 'return' are thus just as suitable for infinitely many repeats only. The criticism expressed against the use of expected values can therefore be levelled also against Holthausen's model. Furthermore, he also rests his decision rule on the EU maxim. As a result of his desire to make the rule comply with the EU principle, his decision rule does not allow any trade-off between favourable and unfavourable results. Also, because the indifference curves are linear in (μ, σ) space, Holthausen's decision rule may fail to recommend diversification of investments in decision situations where a risk-free asset is assumed to exist.

Again, all decision rules discussed in this chapter are based on infinitely many repeats. Either, because they include the expected value to keep them reconcilable with the EU principle, or, because their risk and return measures are calculated using infinitely many repeats of the gambles. They must be diagnosed as incapable of capturing the problems incurred if a gamble is not repeated infinitely often. The true problem of choosing among risky prospects, that is, the problem of forecasting the next outcome of a chance experiment, is disregarded. What can be said about many of the discussed rules is that their attempt to avoid outcomes below a certain target return has without doubt intuitive appeal. But this appeal has to be modelled differently.

Notes

1 This characterisation is far from providing an indisputable and disjunctive classification. No such attempt is made here.
2 This definition is by Schneeweiß (1967). A distribution parameter is a functional assigning a real-valued number to some subset of the sample space.
3 Such an approximation may be based on a Taylor series expansion about the expected value.
4 Roy (1952), p. 432.
5 See Cramér (1930), and Beard et al. (1969).
6 The most prominent example is Graham and Dodd (1934).
7 Example given in Luce and Raiffa (1957).
8 Munier (1988), pp. 1–2.
9 Schneeweiß (1967), pp. 49–50.
10 It was first proven by Khintchine (1929).
11 For a discussion of the misconceptions of the law of large numbers, see Feller (1968), pp. 248–51.
12 These two conditions are common to all versions of the law of large numbers. They cannot be avoided if the law of large numbers is relied on. What can be avoided are special requirements posted by specific versions. For example, Khintchine's version requires the gambles be independent and identically distributed. This requirement may be met by games of chance, but it is hardly met in portfolio choice situations with their ever-changing conditions. For portfolio choice situations, the version of the general weak law of large numbers described in Feller (1968), pp. 253–6, is more apt. It does not postulate common distributions. Since the argument presented in this treatise will rest only on the two conditions common to all versions of the law of large numbers, no distinction between versions is necessary and confusing semantics can be avoided.
13 Krelle (1968), pp. 173–4.
14 Krelle (1968), p. 174.
15 Munier (1988), pp. 1–2.

16 Some authors assume a pay-off of 2^k units of money per trial, which changes the elements of the infinite series to being equal to 1.

17 Cited after the translation of Daniel Bernoulli (1738) by Sommer, pp. 31–5. There seem to be no accounts of the game having actually been played or offered for play.

18 Feller (1968), pp. 262–3. The general case is discussed in Feller (1945).

19 Feller (1968), pp. 252–3.

20 Many others have proposed solutions similar to his, like G. Cramér in 1728, P.R. de Montmort in 1728 and Le Clerc de Buffon in 1730. Overviews are given by Menger (1934), Samuelson (1977) and Shafer (1988).

21 The description given follows Stegmüller (1973), pp. 296–7.

22 Example given in Schneeweiß (1967).

23 Shafer (1988), p. 868.

24 Menger (1934), pp. 483–4, does make this distinction, albeit only verbally. He expresses some doubts about whether the two can be distinguished and quantified in reality, which may have led to von Neumann and Morgenstern combining the two.

25 Example given in Reichling (1996).

26 Linearity suffices, since $\varphi(u)$ is defined up to a linear transformation only.

27 Krelle (1968), pp. 123–9. He mentions being influenced by Luce and Raiffa (1957).

28 Krelle (1968), p. 137.

29 Shoemaker (1982), p. 535.

30 The following classification and description are taken from Munier (1988).

31 A good review is given by Buschena and Zilberman (1994b).

32 It holds good except for those variants that include a transformation of probabilities as well, like Kahneman and Tversky's (1979) 'prospect theory' and Karmarkar's (1974) 'subjectively weighted utility'. These transformed 'probabilities' do not sum up to unity and the preference index assigned thus cannot be regarded as a mathematical expectation of a chance variable. Although probably worth pursuing, these contributions will be disregarded here for the sake of comparability and tractability. Applying transformed probabilities to portfolio choice problems is an entirely different approach from what will be discussed here.

33 Roy (1952), p. 431. As shown in section 3.2, a 'large number' of occasions is not sufficient.

34 Example given in Marschak (1938).

35 The consumption–investment interrelation is briefly sketched in Alexander and Francis (1986), pp. 8–9.

36 Markowitz (1959), p. 48.

37 The following descriptions are partly from Alexander and Francis (1986), pp. 50–65.

38 Markowitz (1952), p. 82.

39 Investments are infinitely divisible, no two assets' returns have a correlation coefficient of $\rho = -1$, no asset has a variance of $V[R] = 0$, no asset's weight x_h must be negative.

40 The shape is derived in, for example, Alexander and Francis (1986), pp. 32–3.

Indifference curves are a standard tool in problems of decision under certainty, with consumption theory being a prominent application.

41 The exception is investors who will always invest in the asset with the highest expected value. It is also possible that the most preferred expected value-to-variance combination is satisfied by a single asset. In general, though, diversification will yield preferred combinations.

42 Of course, situations are conceivable in which diversification is not recommendable. Typically, these are situations of 'all or nothing'. The parameters in Markowitz's decision rule must then be set to yield extreme decisions.

43 Merton (1972).

44 Markowitz (1952), p. 77.

45 It is not surprising that both Bernoulli's rule and $u(r) = r$ imply diminishing marginal utilities of money wealth. Bernoulli argues that the utility of a monetary gain should be inversely proportional to the monetary wealth of the gambler; and yields are calculated by dividing any gain or loss by the amount of money invested.

46 Markowitz (1959), pp. 286–7.

47 See Schneeweiß (1967), pp. 89–98, or Markowitz (1959), p. 287.

48 That the risk preference function has to be quadratic in the returns can also be derived by employing a Taylor series. See, for example, Tobin (1958), or Richter (1959/60).

49 Markowitz (1959), p. 288.

50 Richter (1959/60), p. 155. Ross (1982) shows that under certain assumptions on market behaviour, μ–σ^2 rules may comply with the EU principle even if the 'utility' function is not quadratic and returns are not normally distributed. Since the assumptions are rather stringent, this case is not considered any further.

51 Krelle (1968), pp. 148–59.

52 See, for example, Goldberger (1991), pp. 29–30.

53 Markowitz (1959), p. 52, claims that 'one measure of central tendency is better than another if it generates better efficient portfolios'. This is a void statement, because his definition of 'efficiency' is not independent of the chosen measure of central tendency. Further, 'a comparison of measures can be based either on specific instances or on general principles'. But the general principles he refers to are the von Neumann–Morgenstern axioms of rational behaviour (Markowitz, 1959, Chapters X–XIII) which support neither a specific choice nor a specific combination of parameters.

54 An early treatise is provided by Cramér (1930).

55 Roy (1952), p. 431.

56 Roy (1952), p. 432.

57 Conceptualisations of 'downside risk' are given, for example, in Harlow (1991), and Balzer (1994).

58 Roy (1952), p. 432.

59 Example given in Schneeweiß (1967), pp. 99–100.

60 Example given in Krelle (1968), pp. 131–2.

61 Roy (1952), p. 433.

62 Whether or not such an asset actually exists is not the issue here. But Roy refers to investments made only once, in which case a risk-free return can very well be

assumed, especially if short investment periods are considered. In contrast, it is difficult to justify the assumption that a risk-free asset exists in Markowitz's case, which, as has been argued, implies infinitely many repeats. There would seem to be no asset that guarantees a risk-free return over infinitely many periods.

63 Roy assumes that expected value and variance are the only quantities known to the investor. He has thus to rely on Chebyshev's inequality. Nevertheless, minimisation of $P(R = r \leq d^*)$ should be associated with Roy's safety first rule. Employing Chebyshev's inequality should be separated from the rule itself.

64 Roy (1952), pp. 434–5.

65 Unlike Roy, who applies his decision rule to both net income and percentage returns, Telser considers net income alone. But Telser's analysis may be transformed one-to-one to match decisions made in yield space.

66 Telser (1955/56), p. 2.

67 Telser (1955/56), p. 3. It must be remembered that it is not his prime goal to develop a portfolio choice theory.

68 Kataoka (1963), p. 182.

69 Wald (1950).

70 $P(R = r \leq \xi_\alpha) = \alpha$ becomes $P(R = r \leq \xi_\alpha) = 0$ at $(0, r_f)$ and the distribution collapses.

71 $A(w_T)$ is referred to as the Pratt–Arrow measure of risk aversion. See Pratt (1964). Since Markowitz sets $u(r) = r$, the above definition applies to the risk attitude function as well.

72 For a concise survey and a list of authors, see Alexander and Francis (1986), pp. 26–9.

73 The argument is summarised in Fama (1976).

74 See Feller (1971), p. 260.

75 Both authors cite earlier works on the frequency distribution of price changes and changes in the natural logarithms of prices, which are not restated here in detail.

76 There are several references available for a rigorous discussion of stable Paretian distributions. The definition used here is taken from Feller (1971), pp. 169–70. The general theory was initiated by Lévy (1924, 1937). A mathematical treatment can be found in Gnedenko and Kolmogorov (1954). A concise description is found in Mandelbrot (1963) and Fama (1965a).

77 Fama (1965b), p. 405.

78 Fama (1965b), p. 417.

79 In later publications Fama becomes much more vague about the decision rule. In Fama and Miller (1972), p. 266, it is given as $\Psi(G) = \psi(\mu_R, \sigma_R)$ together with the statement that σ_R 'is no longer the standard deviation'.

80 Lange (1944), pp. 29ff. Many preliminary thoughts are found in Hicks (1939).

81 Fama and Miller (1972), p. 266.

82 Schneeweiß (1967), p. 108. He makes some additional assumptions on the continuity and boundedness of the function $\psi(.)$.

83 Blattberg and Gonedes (1974).

84 Kon (1984).

85 Officer (1972), Hsu et al. (1974) and Hagerman (1978).

86 Fishburn (1977), p. 117. He claims that this contention was set forth by Domar and Musgrave (1944), Markowitz (1959) and Mao (1970a, b).

87 Markowitz (1952).

88 Balzer (1994).
89 Markowitz (1959), p. 287.
90 Markowitz (1959), pp. 209–10.
91 Schneeweiß (1967), pp. 111–13, points out that the theorem given in section 3.4 may be applied to derive the functional form of φ(.) and ψ(.) only if the target return *d* is identical for all gambles. It may not be applied if, for example $d = E[R]$, which would be different for all gambles. No ordinal risk parameter may be chosen that comprises $E[R]$. Thus, although $E[R]$ seems a natural candidate for the target return, the EU principle forbids its use. This is true for all 'risk measures' described in this chapter.
92 Schneeweiß (1967), p. 100.
93 Markowitz (1959), p. 194.
94 Markowitz (1991), p. 374. He lists extensive references on pre-1990 contributions to semi-variance and related quantities on the following pages.
95 A concise list of such arguments can be found in Hogan and Warren (1974), p. 2.
96 Lower partial moments are in turn special cases of a 'risk measure' by Stone (1973).
97 Fishburn (1977), p. 116.
98 Fishburn (1977), p. 116, and Libby and Fishburn (1977), p. 277.
99 The value $d = E[R]$ must again be excluded.
100 Fishburn (1977).
101 Schneeweiß (1967), p. 37, calls this the 'monotony principle'.
102 This formulation goes back to Massé and Morlat (1953). The idea of stochastic dominance goes back to Jacob Bernoulli (1713).
103 Quirk and Saposnik (1962), Fishburn (1964), Hadar and Russel (1969, 1971) and Hanoch and Levy (1969) obtain this rule.
104 Hadar and Russel (1969, 1971) and Hanoch and Levy (1969).
105 Whitmore (1970).
106 The EU principle's combined 'utility' function $\omega(r)$ will for the following analysis again be separated into the risk attitude function $\varphi(u)$ and the utility function $u(r)$. Again, both fall together if $u(r) = r$.
107 Bawa (1978), p. 255.
108 Bawa (1978), pp. 258–9.
109 A theorem for the class of risk attitude functions with decreasing absolute risk aversion is also given, but is applicable only to gambles with equal means.
110 Bawa (1978), p. 257.
111 See Fishburn (1977), p. 117.
112 Accordingly, Schneeweiß (1967), p. 38, refers to first-order stochastic dominance as the 'dominance principle' and considers it a necessary condition for 'rationality', rather than a decision rule.
113 Bawa and Lindenberg (1977), pp. 192–3, and Harlow and Rao (1989), p. 288.
114 Bawa and Lindenberg (1977). Harlow and Rao (1989) do not set the risk-free rate equal to the target return. Their tangent function is not linear in $(\mu, LPM)^{1/n}$ space.

CHAPTER 4

Adequate Decision Rules for Portfolio Choice

4.1 CRITERIA OF ADEQUACY

Normative decision rules are commonly deemed reasonable for decisions under Knightian risk if and only if they comply with the EU principle and obey the EU principle's definition of 'rationality'. This convention has been criticised here. Normative ideals are but mere convictions on how individuals should make a decision, and convictions cannot be justified conclusively. Terms like 'rationality' and 'plausibility', frequently used to justify or refute specific decision rules, are empty phrases. Meaning is given to them solely by opinion. No arguments can be provided to make a decision rule accepted as 'rational' by any two people not sharing the same opinion on rationality, especially no reference to logic or to any framework deducible from it. Discussions on which decision rule should be accepted as 'rational' thus cannot reach any conclusion. Any decision rule may be labelled 'rational' and recommended. Judging decision rules by their congruence with the EU principle is thus futile. There is no reason to necessarily accept the EU principle as the yardstick for 'rationality'.

By the same token, a normative position lacks any justification other than opinion. A normative decision rule can gain approval and acceptance only if the opinion expressed is shared. The simplest way to achieve this is to submit the decision rule to some definition of 'rationality' that has already gained widespread acceptance. This is the reason why almost all portfolio choice rules have recourse to the EU principle. The EU principle's acceptance is simply borrowed.

At times, further acceptance is sought by imposing some additional requirements on the EU principle's risk attitude function, such as decreasing absolute risk aversion as defined by Arrow and Pratt. Claiming that these requirements follow from 'prevalent [...] modes of economic behaviour'[1] is nothing but an attempt to support a normative position with empirical observations, which is another popular way of seeking acceptance. Any such attempt disregards the distinct nature of normative and descriptive decision theory. As has been argued, empirical observations cannot support normative beliefs, just as they cannot falsify them.

Another way of gaining acceptance is to embed the decision rule in a framework of axioms. This is the route followed by the EU principle. The opinion on 'rationality' expressed by the EU principle is thus dissected. Acceptance of the EU principle's definition of 'rationality' can be achieved by discussing the 'rationality' of the axioms, which aids in forming and spreading an opinion. Of course, the axioms cannot provide any objective justification. They are logically equivalent to the principle itself.

Given that normative decision rules lack any justification other than opinion, it is striking that the decision rules prominent in portfolio choice theory today show a distinctive lack of diversity. In all of them, expected values play an important part, either because they are forced to submit themselves to the EU principle, or because they comprise expected values.

The predominance of expected values could, of course, be simply attributable to their mathematical tractability. But there seems to be more to it. Expected values may seek support in the law of large numbers, helping them to gain widespread acceptance. The reasoning is simple. The law of large numbers asserts that after infinitely many repeats the average outcome of a gamble will with probability one be equal to the gamble's expected value. The expected value thus turns into the only likely outcome, and the decision situation may then be treated as if it was one of certainty. It is natural to recommend a decision rule that is concerned solely about the utility of the all but certain outcome. Such a decision rule can thus well be expected to gain widespread approval.

But this line of reasoning is valid only for situations of infinitely many repeats. It may thus be used for the expected gain rule, or for Bernoulli's moral expectation rule. These rules were designed for games of chance, that is, for situations in which infinitely many repeats may be thinkable. However, the expected value's predominance indicates that the support the law of large numbers provides in such situations has been transferred to the expected value itself, without consideration of the situation at hand. It would also not be surprising if it has implicitly been transferred to the EU principle. After all, the EU principle is but an amendment of Bernoulli's moral expectation rule.

It may be worth emphasising that no normative decision rule is refuted in this treatise simply because it employs expected values in situations of no or only finitely many repeats. As has been argued, normative decision rules are based solely on opinion and cannot be refuted. Any argument on expressed opinion is futile. A statement of 'one should' cannot be disputed.

The case that is made here rests on any support that may implicitly or explicitly be attached to an opinion. A statement of 'one should, because ...' may well be disputed for what follows the 'because'. If support is sought for a recommendation, it is fair to ask that this support fit the decision rule and the decision situation in question. If a decision rule is recommended with reference to the law of large numbers, then this recommendation would be acceptable only if the decision situation comprises infinitely many repeats and if nothing but the average result is important.

The recommendations that will be made here are thus not based on some concept of 'rationality'. Their validity for certain decision situations is judged by their 'adequacy' for the specific decision situation under consideration. Of course, 'adequacy' is per se also an empty phrase, just as 'rationality' and 'plausibility' are. It needs to be defined. A definition will be found by looking at the problem of decisions under Knightian risk from the related perspective mentioned in section 3.4, the problem of prediction.

The main feature of decisions under Knightian risk is not that a decision has to be made. The main feature is that the result of any decision is uncertain. The result of the action taken depends on the outcome of a chance experiment. Underneath the decision problem thus lies the problem of predicting one or several outcomes of a chance experiment. A decision rule may thus be recommended on the basis of its predictive quality, or the predictive quality of its components. The decision rule then seeks acceptance through its degree of predictive quality, which needs to be defined. It is natural to define predictive quality in relation to some sort of 'costs' of false prediction. Predictors are then chosen depending on the chosen definition of the 'costs' of false prediction, under the premise that 'costs' are incurred and do matter.

The problem of prediction is omnipresent in classic econometrics. The criterion most commonly used for good prediction is the mean squared forecast error, MSFE for short, defined as $E[(Y-c)^2]$. The term $(Y-c)^2$ thus may be viewed as measuring the 'costs' of bad prediction of a single outcome. The value that minimises the MSFE is the expected value, $E[Y]$, with the MSFE's minimum value being the random variable's variance, $V[Y]$.

Viewed from this perspective, Markowitz's interpretations of 'return' and 'risk' receive new meanings. With the problem of predicting the outcome of a chance experiment in mind, $E[Y]$ is chosen because it minimises the costs of false prediction. $V[Y]$ is chosen because it quantifies the costs' minimum value. Markowitz's μ–σ^2 rule thus evaluates an investment according to what the costs are of badly predicting the investment's outcomes, as measured by the MSFE. But to ensure that both the expected value and the minimum value of the MSFE will actually be obtained, the prediction, that is the gamble or the investment, has to be repeated an infinite number of times. Only then does the law of large numbers ensure that the expected value and the minimum value of the MSFE will be achieved with probability one. The presumption behind the MSFE as a criterion of good prediction is thus that infinitely many repeats are feasible.

The criterion of good prediction that fits most decision rules is more simplistic, however. It may be called the mean forecast error, MFE for short, defined as $E[(Y-c)^2]$. Obviously, it is also the expected value that minimises this criterion, with zero being the minimum value.

That the MFE rather than the MSFE stands behind most decision rules has historical reasons. Decision theory emanated from evaluating games of chance. The expected gain of a gamble was compared to its entrance fee, and a gamble was considered 'fair', if its entrance fee was equal to the expected value of the gain. Behind this concept of 'fairness' stands the notion that a 'fair' gamble should not favour one or the other gambler, and that gains and losses will eventually cancel each other out if the gamble were played often enough.[2] The criterion of balancing gains and losses over many repeats is obviously equivalent to the MFE. If Y is the uncertain result of a gamble, and c its entrance fee, then only $c = E[Y]$ asserts that the mean balance of gains and losses is equal to zero.[3]

The kind of predictive quality of the expected value so defined applies to all decision rules that emanated from the expected gains rule, that is, Bernoulli's rule, Bayes's rule and von Neumann and Morgenstern's expected utility principle. The same is true for all decision rules that were designed to comply with the EU principle's normative maxim.

It is obvious that 'costs' as defined by the MFE or the MSFE can only be applied to decision situations comprising infinitely many repeats. Only then can the law of large numbers be applied to assert that the minimum value of the MFE or the MSFE will be achieved with probability one. If 'adequacy' is now defined by the applicability of the chosen criterion for good prediction to a certain decision situation, then the above decision rules are only 'adequate' for decision situations in which the gamble is repeated an infinite number of times. Only then do the probability limits of the law of large numbers hold exactly.

Finitely many repeats are not sufficient, no matter how many repeats are played, because approximations to the law of large numbers necessitate defining thresholds of perceptibility, one with respect to differences in probabilities, one with respect to differences in results. As Krelle points out, and as has already been mentioned in section 3.2, such thresholds contradict Debreu's axiom of transitivity.[4] But all of Debreu's axioms have to be obeyed, if decision rules are used to reflect preference relations among gambles.

With 'adequacy' defined as above, almost all decision rules prominent in portfolio selection theory today may thus be called 'adequate' only for such Knightian risk situations that are characterised by infinite repetition. This is true for Markowitz's μ–σ^2 rule, because it is based on the MSFE criterion of good prediction. It is also true for all rules that are inspired by or are forced to submit themselves to the EU principle, because the EU principle is based on the MFE criterion.[5] That infinitely many repeats were never questioned is probably again due to the history of decision theory. In games of chance, the first application and main illustration of situations of Knightian risk, the dimension of time and the problem of infinity seem irrelevant, although, as Samuelson concedes, the question always remains of what infinity 'is supposed to mean in a real life situation'.[6]

Within a portfolio selection framework, however, infinitely many repeats may be conceded only for very few decision situations. To illustrate this, it is convenient to characterise investments in real or financial assets or portfolios by their 'investment period', the time period over which an investment yields or is perceived to yield a return. Investment periods may be defined as being subperiods of the 'investment horizon', which may then be defined as the time span over which an investment is planned to be upheld.[7] An investor finds him- or herself in a decision situation under Knightian risk only at the beginning of an 'investment horizon'. This corresponds to a gambling situation in which a single gamble marks the beginning and end of the investment period, and where the number of times the gamble is played defines the investment horizon.

Infinitely many repetitions of an investment, that is, infinitely many investment periods, are feasible only in two cases. Either the investment horizon is itself infinite, which would allow dividing it into infinitely many investment periods of finite length, or the investment horizon is finite, but divided into infinitely many investment periods of no positive length. These are the only investment situations to which a decision rule based on infinitely many repeats may be applied.

The latter situation seems irrelevant, because no actual investment, just as no actual gamble, yields a return instantly. No recommendation is needed for irrelevant situations. The former situation is one that only very few investors may find themselves in. It seems plausible only for institutional investors, whose life span is not limited by nature. More common investment situations are either characterised by a single investment decision, or by a finite investment horizon, like a natural lifetime, or the time to retirement, which is dividable into periods of positive length, like weeks, months or years. For these decision situations, most of the decision rules discussed in Chapter 3 are inadequate.

Only two of the discussed decision rules are adequate for gambles played only once. The safety first rules of Roy and Kataoka are specifically designed for single-period investment decisions, and do not have recourse to any expected value. Unfortunately, Roy and Kataoka disregard any possible trade-off between accepting higher probabilities of an unfavourable result for higher probabilities of a favourable result. This lack of any possible trade-off must be criticised. It means recommending peculiar behaviour if a risk-free investment alternative is added to the decision situation envisaged by Roy and Kataoka. Clearly, single-period decision situations are not described adequately without a risk-free asset, regardless of the length of the investment period.[8]

The objective of the following sections is to recommend decision rules that are 'adequate' for specific decision situations. 'Adequacy' will be based on a definition of predictive quality that may be applied to the specific decision situation. At the same time, the decision rules will be required to recommend diversification behaviour. The ability to recommend diversification is deemed reasonable. Since the ability to explain diversification behaviour may also be viewed, indeed has been viewed, as an acid test for descriptive validity, the following analyses do carry some risk of blurring the distinction between normative and descriptive decision theory. But the following decision rules are meant as recommendations, that is, as normative rules. They are neither seen as descriptively valid, nor are they tested empirically. This is not least to acknowledge that any decision rule's foundations, that is, Debreu's axioms, have been empirically falsified, as mentioned in section 2.2.

4.2 DECISION RULES ADEQUATE FOR SINGLE-PERIOD INVESTMENTS

A decision rule can only be 'adequate' for single gambles, if the criterion for good prediction that it is based on is applicable to single chance experiments. Criteria relying on mathematical expectations, like the MSE and the MSFE, have been shown to be adequate only for infinitely often repeated chance experiments. Criteria for good prediction of a chance experiment's single next outcome must be based on other quantities.

One alternative is to rely on the distribution's quantiles, that is, on probabilities. Quite clearly, probabilities may be applied to situations involving single or finitely often repeated gambles. An example of such a criterion is to minimise the probability of false prediction, that is, to maximise $P(Y-c=0)$. In the case of discrete sample spaces, this criterion leads to choosing the mode of Y as predictor.[9] Of course, the mode cannot be employed in a portfolio choice situation if returns are modelled by continuous distributions. The mode's inappropriateness to such situations notwithstanding, the reasoning given above leads to the suggestion that decision rules adequate for single or finitely often repeated gambles should be based on probabilities rather than on moments.

Having recourse to probabilities is by no means a novel idea, of course. Quite a few authors have proposed decision rules that rely, in part at least, on quantiles rather than on moments. Among those who recommend using quantiles together with the expected value is Fama (1965b), whose recommendation was discussed in section 3.6. Fama proposes a decision rule comprising the expected value and the intersextile range. Baumol (1968) proposes a decision rule comprising the expected value and a lower confidence limit. Markowitz (1959) discusses the probability of loss as a possible measure for risk. Authors that recommend decision rules relying solely on quantiles and probabilities are Roy (1952) and Kataoka (1963), whose recommendations were discussed in section 3.5. Another example is Lange (1944), although his recommendation is somewhat implicit. For situations characterised by continuous distributions, Lange recommends using the median and the distribution's interquartile range. These parameters are often used to quantify central tendency and dispersion of distributions along an ordinal scale.

The rule proposed by Lange is indeed adequate for single or finitely often repeated decision situations. The only objection is that the median and the interquartile range partly cover the same possible results. If, as seems natural, the median is chosen as the protagonist within the decision rule, and the interquartile range as the antagonist, then some results are valued positively and negatively by the same token. Holthausen (1981) objects to using the expected value together with any LPM as the measure for 'risk' in a similar fashion. 'Since outcomes below the target outcome have already been considered in the risk measure …, it seems redundant if not contradictory to include them in the return measure.'[10]

The recommendation made here for single gambles and single-period investments is to use not one but two percentage points. The first should be chosen so that it indicates which results are considered unfavourable. The second should be chosen so that it indicates which results are considered favourable. Due to the subjectivity inherent in any decision problem, the terms 'favourable' and 'unfavourable' must refer to the utilities assigned to the possible results of the investment, not to the results themselves.

Following Roy, let d^* and d^{**} denote values of an investment's return distribution, R_i. Let d^* denote the highest percentage return that is still considered unfavourable. Let d^{**} denote the lowest percentage return that is still considered favourable. Let these percentage points have assigned utilities $\delta_1 = u(d^*)$ and $\delta_2 = u(d^{**})$. δ_1 and δ_2 are then values of the utility distribution associated with the investment's possible results, U_i. In the decision rule recommended here, the probability of a utility higher than δ_2 takes on the role of the protagonist, while the probability of a utility lower than δ_1 takes on the role of the antagonist. In short, the decision rule recommended for single-period portfolio choice situations is

$$\Psi(G) = \psi\big(P(U - u > \delta_2), P(U = u < \delta_1)\big) = \psi\big(1 - F(\delta_2), F(\delta_1)\big)$$

Because it comprises two cumulative probabilities, it will be referred to as the 'CP rule'. The name is admittedly neither elegant nor self-explanatory, but it does help avoid cumbersome wording.

Which percentage points are chosen depends on the individual's subjective definition of favourable and unfavourable results in a given decision situation. The percentage points define what may be called 'target utilities', both on the upside and the downside. They may, of course, fall together, or even reverse order such that $\delta_2 < \delta_1$, although this latter case would fall under the above-mentioned critique levelled by Holthausen against combining the expected value with some *LPM*.

The functional relation between the two probabilities may be chosen such that it captures any subjective degree of 'risk aversion', with 'risk aversion' left to be defined. It is plausible to define a 'risk averse' investor as someone who accepts an increase in the probability of unfavourable returns only for a certain increase in the probability of favourable returns. How much increase in $(1–F(\delta_2))$ is wanted for any given increase in $F(\delta_1)$ depends on the decision rule's specification in a given situation.

Exact relations between $(1–F(\delta_2))$ and $F(\delta_1)$ need not be specified here, just as specific values for δ_1 and δ_2 need not be. Only for specifically defined situations is it necessary to cast $(1–F(\delta_2))$ and $F(\delta_1)$ into a mathematical function, to define parameters of that function, or to define 'risk aversion' with respect to such parameters. 'Risk seeking' behaviour and 'risk neutral' behaviour could then also be defined.

Such definitions are not given here for two reasons. First, the focus here is not on recommendations for specific decision situations but on adequate decision rules in general. Specific recommendations may be given when specific situations are at stake. Second, such definitions help to entrench the notion that 'risk' is measurable by a single entity. In contrast to other decision rules, especially those that combine the expected value with some 'measure of risk', the two entities $(1–F(\delta_2))$ and $F(\delta_1)$ are not seen as completely separate and independent. Whatever quantiles are chosen, they simply mark which returns are considered 'favourable' and 'unfavourable', without obscuring the fact that the underlying distribution is the cause of the risk involved in the decision. A decision rule should clearly state that risk is a characteristic feature of the decision situation. Of course, under brute force the CP rule will still submit to the appeal of the dichotomy into 'risk' and 'return'. Those looking for a measure of risk will find it in $F(\delta_1)$. The CP rule is thus also intuitive, but intuitive appeal is not of primary concern.

It is hardly conceivable that as yet such a simple decision rule has not been recommended.[11] One explanation might be that the CP rule does not comply with the EU principle. This would also very likely be the first critique levelled against it by the EU principle's proponents. But the role assigned to the EU principle by its proponents, the role of guardian of 'rationality', has been refuted here. The CP rule's compliance with the EU principle is considered completely irrelevant.

Another critique frequently levelled against probability-based decision rules is that the entire distribution of all gambles needs to be 'known'. It is implied that decision rules relying on moments necessitate 'knowledge' of the relevant moments only. This objection is not valid here, because portfolio choice theory is handled as a special case of decisions under Knightian risk. These situations are characterised by the assumption that the individual feels able to attach probabilities to all possible results of his or her action. Knowledge of the underlying distribution is thus presumed. To object to this assumption is to alter the problem. If it is presumed that the underlying distributions and probabilities are unknown, portfolio choice problems turn from being problems of decision under Knightian risk to being problems of statistical decision. Such problems are not considered here.[12]

A graphical analysis of the CP rule will now be given. It seems advantageous to conduct this graphical analysis in exactly the same setting as was used in sections 3.4 and 3.5. The CP rule can then be compared directly to Markowitz's μ–σ^2 rule and to the safety first rules discussed. Roy (1952) has recourse to Chebyshev's inequality to provide an easily comprehensible graphical analysis of his safety first rule. His example will be followed here.

Chebyshev's inequality provides upper bounds for cumulative probabilities on the basis of expected values and variances only. It thus allows the depiction of probability-based decision rules in (μ, σ) space, irrespective of the underlying distributions in a specific situation. It is important to remember that Chebyshev's inequality is not an integral part of Roy's safety first rule. Neither is it an integral part of the CP rule. Chebyshev's inequality is used for illustrative purposes only. The Knightian risk setting presumes that probabilities can be attached to all possible results. Relying entirely on Chebyshev's inequality is unnecessary in this setting. To do so would restrict the decision rule's applicability to situations in which the results' distributions have finite variances. It may also lead to decisions that would not have been made had the distributions' entire information been used, since any information other than expected values and variances is disregarded.

But employing Chebyshev's inequality for illustrative purposes involves no risk. It demonstrates that the CP rule is adequate for single-period portfolio choice situations irrespective of specific distributions. This is also true if no finite variances exist.

Since all results need to be evaluated by the decision-making individual, the decision rule should be depicted in (μ_U, σ_U) space, rather than in (μ_R, σ_R) space. To achieve comparability, it will be assumed that the $u(r)$ are cardinal utilities that are functions of the returns alone and additive. Under these assumptions, the expected value and the standard deviation of the utility of a portfolio can be calculated in the same manner as the expected value and the standard deviation of the return of a portfolio. The shape of the efficient set is then similar in (μ_U, σ_U) space and in (μ_R, σ_R) space. If no risk-free asset exists, the 'efficient set' of portfolios is then concave in (μ_U, σ_U) space. If a risk-free asset exists, as should be assumed for single-period portfolio choice situations, the efficient set of portfolios is a ray emanating from the point (0, $u(r_f)$).

Minimising the probability of an unfavourable result, that is, minimising $P(u(R) = u(r) < \delta_1)$, is equal to maximising the slope of a ray emanating from the point $(0, \delta_1)$, as Chebyshev's inequality will reveal. Maximising the probability of a favourable result, that is, maximising $P(u(R) = u(r) > \delta_2)$, is equal to minimising $P(u(R) = u(r) < \delta_2)$, and thus equal to maximising the slope of a ray emanating from the point $(0, \delta_2)$.

Figure 4.1 illustrates how the most preferred portfolio is identified by the CP rule in the case that no risk-free asset exists. The efficient set of portfolios is again found on the curve between points *A* and *B*. The ray labelled d_1 indicates the upper bound of $P(u(R) = u(r) < \delta_1)$, that is, of the probability of an unfavourable result. The ray labelled d_2 indicates the probability of a utility less than δ_2, that is, the probability of a result falling short of the 'favourable' level.

The steeper the slope of d_1, the lower the probability of an unfavourable result, while the steeper the slope of d_2, the higher the

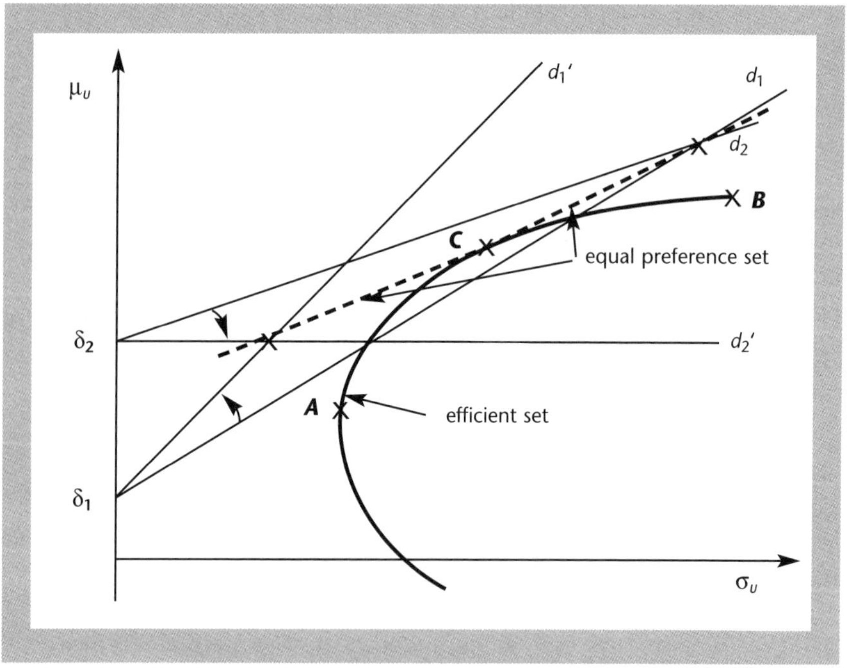

Figure 4.1 Portfolio choice with the CP rule

probability of a favourable result. The steeper both rays are, the more preferred a portfolio is.

Points of intersection of d_1 and d_2 identify portfolios with a specific combination of 1–$F(\delta_2)$ and $F(\delta_1)$. The locations of portfolios that the individual values equally depend on the trade-off between 1–$F(\delta_2)$ and $F(\delta_1)$ specified in the individual's decision rule. If the investor seeks an increase in 1–$F(\delta_2)$ for an increase in $F(\delta_1)$, which may be regarded as 'risk aversion', the trade-off between 1–$F(\delta_2)$ and $F(\delta_1)$ will result in the rays turning in opposite directions when equally valued portfolios are identified. A decrease in the slope of d_1 is acceptable to the investor only if the slope of d_2 simultaneously increases, with the decision rule, or the 'degree of risk aversion', determining by how much.

Simultaneous turning of the rays d_1 and d_2 in accordance with the specific decision rule thus allows construction of sets that indicate equal levels of preference, equivalent to an indifference curve. The slopes of these sets again depend on the specifications of the decision rule, or the 'degree of risk aversion'. The most preferred portfolio is found where a set of equally valued portfolios touches the set of efficient portfolios. Thus, the CP rule is capable of identifying the most preferred portfolio from the feasible set of all conceivable portfolios, while being adequate for single-period decision situations.

The CP rule does also recommend diversification behaviour if a risk-free asset exists. For $\delta_1 < u(r_f) < \delta_2$, a diversified portfolio will be chosen from the efficient set. This case is depicted in Figure 4.2. Of course, if the investor values $u(r_f)$ above all else, he or she is willing to forgo any opportunity of receiving a utility higher than $u(r_f)$. The ray d_1 would then have to be drawn as a vertical line.

For $\delta_1 < \delta_2 < u(r_f)$, the investor will also invest only in the risk-free asset, since this behaviour guarantees a return considered favourable. For $u(r_f) < \delta_1 < \delta_2$, the investor will choose a diversified portfolio, with the amount invested in the risk-free asset again depending on the specifications of the decision rule. Thus, in contrast to Roy's and Kataoka's safety first rules, the CP rule recommends choosing diversified portfolios in all single-period investment situations.

Only if δ_1 and δ_2 coincide are there situations in which the CP rule may fail to recommend holding diversified portfolios. $\delta_1 = \delta_2$ translates into fixing the trade-off between 1–$F(\delta_2)$ and $F(\delta_1)$. This means forfeiting the additional information the CP rule utilises. It means turning it into Roy's safety first rule.

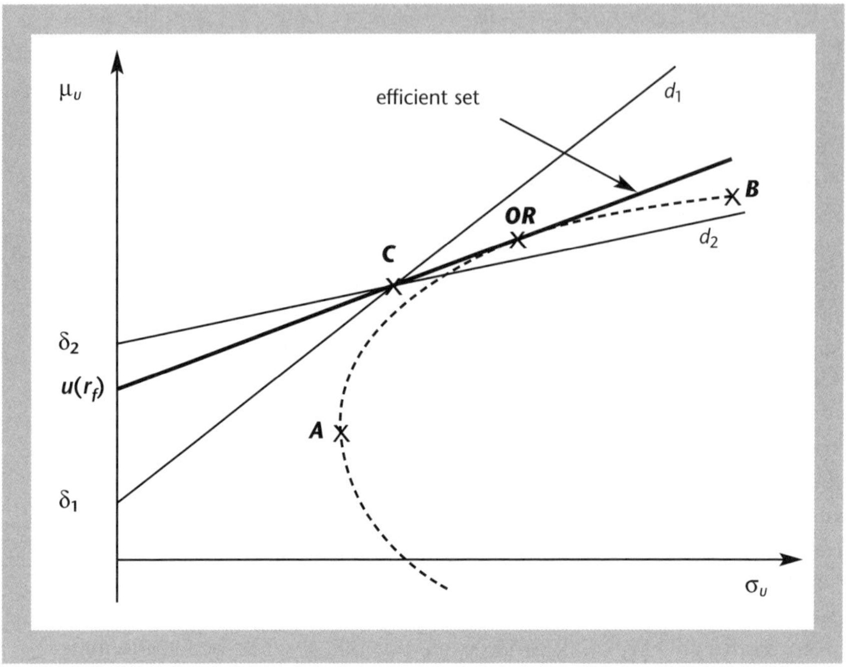

Figure 4.2 Portfolio choice with the CP rule with a risk-free asset

4.3 DECISION RULES ADEQUATE FOR FINITELY OFTEN REPEATED INVESTMENTS

Decision situations in which the same gamble is played several times in a row are common in the field of games of chance. They are also conceivable in the field of portfolio choice, where they have been treated under the label 'multi-period decisions'. The characteristic feature of a multi-period portfolio choice situation is that the investment horizon splits into several investment periods. For example, a chosen portfolio may be planned to be held for one year, but is seen as rendering a return after each month of that year. The investment horizon then comprises twelve investment periods. If the assets' distributions do not change, and if exactly the same portfolio is held at the beginning of each month, then each month's return resembles one trial's pay-off in a sequence of twelve trials of the same gamble.

The decision situation treated in this section is that of choosing a portfolio for a finite investment horizon, which in turn consists of a finite number of investment periods. The decision which portfolio to hold, that is, which weights to assign to all conceivable assets, is made at the beginning of the investment horizon. The decision is not reconsidered after each investment period. Only after the entire investment horizon is the individual confronted with a new decision situation and must select a new portfolio.

Recommendations have been made to base such multi-period decisions on the EU principle.[13] But, as will be shown, decision rules employing moments are just as inadequate for multi-period investment situations as they are for single-period investment situations. Finitely many repeats of a gamble are not sufficient to rely explicitly or implicitly on the law of large numbers.

Multi-period decision situations must be defined sufficiently to facilitate recommending an 'adequate' decision rule. Merely to distinguish between investment horizon and investment period is insufficient. As has been stated in section 2.1, situations of Knightian risk are defined by four different sets: the set of actions, **A**, the set of states of nature, **N**, and the set of all conceived utilities, **U**, which is defined over the set of results, **R**. Single-period and multi-period decision situations differ first and foremost in the possible definitions of the set of results.

For single-period portfolio choice situations, results in this treatise are defined as percentage returns. Other definitions, like absolute returns, or final wealth, are possible, of course. They are simple one-to-one transformations of percentage returns, if initial wealth is seen as given. Single-period decision situations do not change conceptually, whether results are defined as absolute returns, or as final wealth, or as percentage returns. Cardinal utilities are in any case defined only up to a positive linear transformation. The only good argument for choosing percentage returns is that they bring to mind the inherent time dimension of any investment decision, which is why they were chosen here to define investment results in single-period portfolio choice situations.

In multi-period portfolio choice situations, the definition of 'results' and thus of the sets **R** and **U** is not so straightforward. Any gamble that is played repeatedly generates several different kinds of result. One such result is the average gain of the sequence of trials, another is the gain accumulated over the entire sequence, and yet another is the gambler's interim wealth after each trial.

Different kinds of result may thus be used. They capture different perceptions of a decision situation. In situations of portfolio choice both final and interim results may be important to the investor. The decision situation thus needs to be specified with respect to which kind of results are or should be considered important in making an investment decision.

It is conceivable that the investor is or should be concerned only about the final return at the end of the sequence of trials, that is, after the end of the investment horizon. He or she might not or need not care about interim results. It is quite obvious that such a multi-period decision situation is equivalent to the single-period situation treated in section 4.2. After all, the sequence of investments may be combined into one overall investment, with one final result.

Thus, the same decision rule as in section 4.2 may be recommended, comprising the probabilities $P(u(R_T) = u(r_T) > \delta_2)$ and $P(u(R_T) = u(r_T) < \delta_1)$. The suffix T is to indicate that the entire investment horizon is treated as a single period. It is unnecessary to assume that the distribution of the final results and their utilities can actually be calculated from the distribution of the single periods, since situations of Knightian risk are characterised by the individual feeling able to attach probabilities to all possible results of his or her action. The way in which the individual arrives at the probabilities of the final results is of no concern.

Chebyshev's inequality may again be employed for graphical analysis, which remains unchanged as well. The efficient set can be calculated and depicted in $(\mu_{U,T}, \sigma_{U,T})$ space. This set is again linear, if an asset is assumed to exist that generates a risk-free return over the entire investment horizon, and if utilities are assumed cardinal and additive. The slopes of the two rays emanating from $(0, \delta_1)$ and $(0, \delta_2)$ will again indicate upper and lower bounds for the probabilities $P(u(R_T) = u(r_T) < \delta_1)$ and $P(u(R_T) = u(r_T) > \delta_2)$, and will again identify the most preferred portfolio.

But decision situations in which the investor should not focus on final percentage returns alone are also conceivable. In the field of games of chance, the time-honoured example for such a situation is that of a gambler who faces the possibility that during the planned sequence of trials his or her total wealth falls below the minimum amount needed to continue with the gamble. If his or her wealth falls below this amount, he or she is forced to prematurely terminate the sequence of trials. This is the well-known 'gambler's ruin problem', which has a long history in probability theory.[14] Clearly, a decision rule based on final returns alone would not cover all relevant aspects of this situation.

Forced premature termination may also overshadow portfolio choice situations. An investor might need to account for the possibility of having to withdraw his or her investment before the end of the investment horizon. A portfolio manager might face losing his mandate as soon as the portfolio's value falls below a certain percentage of the initial amount received for managing.

In both cases, the threat of forced premature termination leads to the conclusion that interim wealth should receive attention. Results should thus not be defined in terms of final returns alone, but also in terms of interim results. At least two sets of results thus need to be specified to design a decision rule for situations of forced premature termination. The same is true for situations of voluntary premature termination. Optional stopping, as it is sometimes called, is another decision situation where more than just final results must receive consideration. Since no exhaustive treatise of all possible situations can be given here, adequate decision rules shall be exemplified only for portfolio choice situations, which are characterised by forced premature termination.[15]

Defining the set of final results for multi-period portfolio choice situations is still straightforward. Final percentage returns are still the natural choice. The reasoning in favour of final percentage returns still applies. There is no need to turn to other variables instead.

With respect to interim wealth, denoted W_t, several different sets of results can be plausible, depending on the investor's situation or, more accurately, on his or her perception of it. W_t produces a sequence of realisations, one for each period. One or several elements of this sequence may be used to define sets of interim results.

In the classic gambler's ruin problem, the gambler's W_t must not fall below the amount needed to participate in the gamble. A new trial may only be conducted if the preceding trial did not result in wealth falling below the level of entry, here denoted w^*. The definition of the set of interim results and their utilities should thus be based on the events

$$(\{W_1 = w_1 < w^*\}, \{W_2 = w_2 < w^* \mid w_1 > w^*\}, ..., \{W_{\tau-1} = w_{\tau-1} < w^* \mid w_1, w_2, ... w_{\tau-2} > w^*\})$$

or their corresponding complementary events. This situation resembles that of a portfolio manager who loses his or her mandate as soon as the managed portfolio's value falls below w^*. The exact level is of no concern here. It is open for subjective specification. It does not necessarily have to be equivalent to total loss of wealth.

In the other example given above, the situation in which the investor might have to withdraw his or her investment prematurely due to reasons not directly linked to the actual level of wealth, the base for defining the set of interim results and their utilities is the events $\{W_t = w_t < w^*\}$, $t = 1, 2,..., \tau-1$, or, again, their complementary events.

When 'results' have been identified, their sets defined, and utilities applied, decision rules may be designed. Decision rules assign a preference index to each gamble on the base of some parameters of the U_i's associated with the gambles. It has been argued in this treatise that the choice of parameters to use in a decision rule must meet the standard of 'adequacy' defined in section 4.1. The implication of this standard is that usage of any expected value within a decision rule is adequate only if the gamble is repeated an infinite number of times. Only then can the law of large numbers be applied to the average of the results of the trials. It is thus quite obvious that in decision situations consisting of finitely often repeated gambles, the random variables defined over the sets of results and their utilities are not adequately considered by any expected value. This is true even if the average of all results is all that is considered important by the gambler, as has been explained in section 4.1.

It is also true in the two example portfolio choice situations mentioned above, in which final percentage returns and some events regarding interim wealth are considered important. The random variable 'final percentage return', R_T, will see one realisation only, no matter how often the investment will actually be repeated. The random variable interim wealth, W_t, is a function of the preceding wealth, W_{t-1}, meaning that $\{W_t\}$ is a stochastic process whose elements are not independent, even if the period returns R_t are. The sequence of realisations $\{w_1, w_2, ..., w_\tau\}$ is therefore but one realisation of a stochastic process. Events defined on the basis of any elements of this stochastic process will thus also occur only once.

Thus, the variables declared of concern in the above examples, R_T and W_t, and their respective utilities, $u(R_T)$ and $u(W_t)$, will see only one realisation each. One realisation is insufficient to rely on the predictive quality of the expected value in designing a decision rule. The predictive quality of the expected value as defined by the MFE or the MSFE rests on infinitely many repeats and realisations of the random variable in question. To rely on the MFE or the MSFE, infinitely many realisations of R_T and $\{W_t\}$ would be needed. This would require that the stochastic process itself be repeated in its entirety an infinite number of times. Such a situation is hardly imaginable and will not be dealt with here. Following the reasoning of section 4.2, it is conclusive that in situations of finitely many repeats, both kinds of results, final percentage return and any event based on interim wealth, are adequately considered by applying probabilities.

Final percentage returns are adequately considered by the probabilities of $u(R_T)$ falling below some value δ_1, or surpassing some value δ_2. This is the same recommendation that was made for single-period decision situations. It simply derives from the similarity of the two decision situations with regard to final results. With regard to interim wealth, it is also its probability that should receive consideration in the decision rule. This is implied by the above reasoning, no matter what event is defined as an 'interim result' in a given situation.

In the first portfolio choice situation mentioned above, the event of interim wealth falling below level w^* in any period for the first time terminates the sequence of investments. For this decision situation, the probability

$$P(\{W_1 = w_1 < w^*\} \cup \{W_2 = w_2 < w^* \mid w_1 > w^*\} \cup \ldots \cup \{W_{\tau-1} = w_{\tau-1} < w^* \mid w_1, w_2, \ldots, w_{\tau-2} > w^*\})$$

should enter the decision rule. It is unnecessary to assign utilities to the levels of wealth, because the threat inherent in forced premature termination is independent of the utility assigned to the result itself. Of course, since any result has an assigned utility, the above probability could also be stated in terms of $u(W_t)$. The event $\{W_\tau = w_\tau < w \mid w_1, w_2, \ldots, W_{\tau-1} > w^*\}$ need not be included, since no investment is made after period τ. $P(u(R_T) = u(r_T) < \delta_1)$ already takes care of an unfavourable result after period τ.

In the second portfolio choice situation mentioned above, forced premature termination is not governed directly by interim wealth. For this decision situation, the recommendation is that the probability

$$P(\{u(W_1) = u(w_1) < u(w^*)\} \cup \{u(W_2) = u(w_2) < u(w^*)\} \cup \ldots \cup \{u(W_{\tau-1}) = u(w_{\tau-1}) < u(w^*)\})$$

should enter the decision rule. Here the events must be stated in utility terms, since a specific interim result does not force the individual to terminate the sequence. Rather, the intention is to avoid interim results that are considered unfavourable, just in case the investment has to be withdrawn prematurely. The event $\{u(W_\tau) = u(w_\tau) < u(w^*)\}$ may again be excluded, since $P(u(R_T) = u(r_T) < \delta_1)$ takes care of an unfavourable result after period τ.

There are two ways to compose a decision rule from these three probabilities. One way is to include the probabilities of unfavourable interim wealth events as a third parameter, allowing for trade-offs with $P(u(R_T) = u(r_T) < \delta_1)$ and $P(u(R_T) = u(r_T) > \delta_2)$. The other way is to separately use some pre-set probability of interim wealth events as a necessary condition for any asset or portfolio to be part of the efficient set. This possibility arises because, as has been shown in the previous chapter, the two probabilities $P(u(R_T) = u(r_T) < \delta_1)$ and $P(u(R_T) = u(r_T) > \delta_2)$ suffice to unambiguously determine a single portfolio among the efficient set of portfolios.

Which way is chosen to compose the decision rule depends again on the investor's subjective perception of the decision situation. No general recommendation can be given. Using fixed probabilities as a necessary condition seems easier to administer, but that is not a good criterion. Trade-offs between three different probabilities do not seem unmanageable. If probabilities regarding interim wealth events are viewed as a necessary condition for any asset or portfolio to be part of the efficient set, the decision rules recommended for situations of finitely often repeated investments under the thread of forced premature termination are given as

$$\Psi(G) = \psi\big(P\big(u(R_T) = u(r_T) > \delta_2\big), P\big(u(R_T) = u(r_T) < \delta_1\big)\big) = \psi\big(1 - F_T(\delta_2), F_T(\delta_1)\big)$$

n.b. $P(\{W_{G,1} = w_{G,1} < w^*\} \cup \{W_{G,2} = w_{G,2} < w^* \mid w_{G,1} > w^*\} \cup \ldots$
$\cup \{W_{G,\tau-1} = w_{G,\tau-1} < w^* \mid w_{G,1}, w_{G,2}, \ldots, w_{G,\tau-2} > w^*\}) < \alpha$

when premature termination is forced by the level of wealth, and as

$$\Psi(G) = \psi\big(P\big(u(R_T) = u(r_T) > \delta_2\big), P\big(u(R_T) = u(r_T) < \delta_1\big)\big) = \psi\big(1 - F_T(\delta_2), F_T(\delta_1)\big)$$

n.b. $P(\{u(W_{G,1}) = u(w_{G,1}) < u(w^*)\} \cup \{u(W_{G,2}) = u(w_{G,2}) < u(w^*)\} \cup \ldots$
$\cup \{u(W_{G,\tau-1}) = u(w_{G,\tau-1}) < u(w^*)\}) < \alpha$

when premature termination is forced by events not directly linked to interim wealth.

Unfortunately, the two decision rules do not lend themselves to graphical analysis quite as willingly as the previous ones. With the help of Chebyshev's inequality, decision rules comprising only $P(u(R_T) = u(r_T) < \delta_1)$ and $P(u(R_T) = u(r_T) > \delta_2)$ could still easily be depicted in $(\mu_{U,T}, \sigma_{U,T})$ space. The efficient set of risky portfolios and its combinations with the risk-free asset take the same geometrical form as in the graphical analyses given in previous chapters. Ray's emanating from $(0, \delta_1)$ and $(0, \delta_2)$ indicate portfolios that minimise or maximise the respective probabilities.

But Chebychev's inequality cannot be applied in the same manner to identify the portfolios that minimise the probabilities

$$P(\{W_1 = w_1 < w^*\} \cup \{W_2 = w_2 < w^* \mid w_1 > w^*\} \cup \ldots \cup \{W_{\tau-1} = w_{\tau-1} < w^* \mid w_1, w_2, \ldots, w_{\tau-2} > w^*\})$$

and

$$P(\{u(W_1) = u(w_1) < u(w^*)\} \cup \{u(W_2) = u(w_2) < u(w^*)\} \cup \ldots \cup \{u(W_{\tau-1}) = u(w_{\tau-1}) < u(w^*)\})$$

in $(\mu_{U,T}, \sigma_{U,T})$ space. Both probabilities depend in the end on the marginal and conditional distributions of R_t. To identify the portfolios that minimise these probabilities in $(\mu_{U,T}, \sigma_{U,T})$ space without the help of Chebyshev's inequality, a generally valid relation between R_t, W_t and R_T is needed, which does not, however, exist. To apply Chebyshev's inequality, generally valid relations between expected values and conditional expected values, and between variances and conditional variances of R_t, V_t and R_T are needed, which also do not exist. Suffice it to note that even if the R_t are assumed to be independently distributed,

$$V[R_t] = V\left[\prod_{t=1}^{\tau}(1+R_t)\right]$$

which precludes any precise inference from $V[R_t]$ to $V[R_T]$ without making further assumptions. It would presumably be possible to arrive at a special case of a relation between R_t, W_t and R_T by making an assumption on the common distribution of $\{R_1, R_2, \ldots, R_t\}$ and thus of $\{u(R_1), u(R_2), \ldots, u(R_\tau)\}$. But such assumptions have not been made so far, since the analysis of special cases is not the purpose of this treatise. Thus nor will they be made now.

A graphical demonstration may still at least be sketched without having to assume a specific distribution for R_t and $u(R_t)$. It will be given for the decision rule recommended for the second example situation. It is assumed that forced premature termination is caused by events not linked to the level of wealth.

$$P(\{u(W_1) = u(w_1) < u(w^*)\} \cup \{u(W_2) = u(w_2) < u(w^*)\} \cup \ldots \cup \{u(W_{\tau-1}) = u(w_{\tau-1}) < u(w^*)\})$$

will be fixed to α, and treated as a necessary condition for an asset or a portfolio to be an element of the efficient set.

The set of all assets and portfolios that meet this necessary condition shall be called here the 'admissible set'. Only the lower border of the admissible set needs to be depicted. The starting point of this border is easy to determine. It is located close to the point $(0, u(w^*))$. It is not located exactly at this point, if zero variance is indicative of a degenerate distribution.[16] If the monotony principle applies to the utilities assigned to the results, that is, if $u(r_1) > u(r_2)$ if and only if $r_1 > r_2$, then the lower border of the admissible set cannot be horizontal. An increase in $V[R_T]$ must correspond to an increase in $V[R_t]$ and thus to an increase in the probability of wealth falling below w^* in any given period, if $E[R_T]$ and thus $E[R_t]$ do not increase appropriately.

For the same reason the border can never be downward sloping. This would presume that there could be two portfolios with the same $E[R_T]$, and thus the same $E[R_t]$, and with the same probability of their wealth falling below w^* in any period, but with one having a greater $V[R_T]$, and thus $V[R_t]$, than the other.

Also, the lower border of the admissible set is presumably not linear in $(\mu_{U,T}, \sigma_{U,T})$ space. This is obvious when looking at the probability

$$P(\{u(W_1) = u(w_1) < u(w^*)\} \cup \{u(W_2) = u(w_2) < u(w^*)\} \cup \ldots \cup \{u(W_{\tau-1}) = u(w_{\tau-1}) < u(w^*)\})$$

$$= 1-[P(u(W_1) > u(w^*)) \cdot P(u(W_2) > u(w^*) \mid u(W_1) > w^*) \cdot P(u(W_3) > u(w^*) \mid u(W_1) \cap u(W_2) > u(w^*)) \cdot \ldots \cdot P(u(W_{\tau-1}) > u(w^*) \mid u(W_1) \cap u(W_2) \cap \ldots \cap u(W_{\tau-2}) > u(w^*))]$$

with Chebyshev's inequality in mind. First, the conditional expected values and variances of R_t, on which this probability depends, are affected simultaneously by changes in $E[R_t]$ and $V[R_t]$. Second, these changes affect the probability in a multiplicative manner. Third, $E[R_t]$ and $V[R_t]$ do not interact linearly with $E[R_T]$ and $V[R_T]$.

Thus, the lower border of the admissible set is in general not linear in $(\mu_{U,T}, \sigma_{U,T})$ space. Since it also cannot be horizontal or downward sloping, it may be presumed upward sloping as sketched in Figure 4.3. The exact location and slope will depend on the values of $u(w^*)$ and α, and the common distribution of all $u(R_t)$, $t = 1, 2, \ldots, \tau-1$. In Figure 4.3 the efficient set and the lower border of the admissible set are drawn to demonstrate their interaction. All assets above the lower border of the admissible set satisfy

$$P(\{u(W_1) = u(w_1) < u(w^*)\} \cup \{u(W_2) = u(w_2) < u(w^*)\} \cup \ldots \cup \{u(W_{\tau-1}) = u(w_{\tau-1}) < u(w^*)\}) < \alpha$$

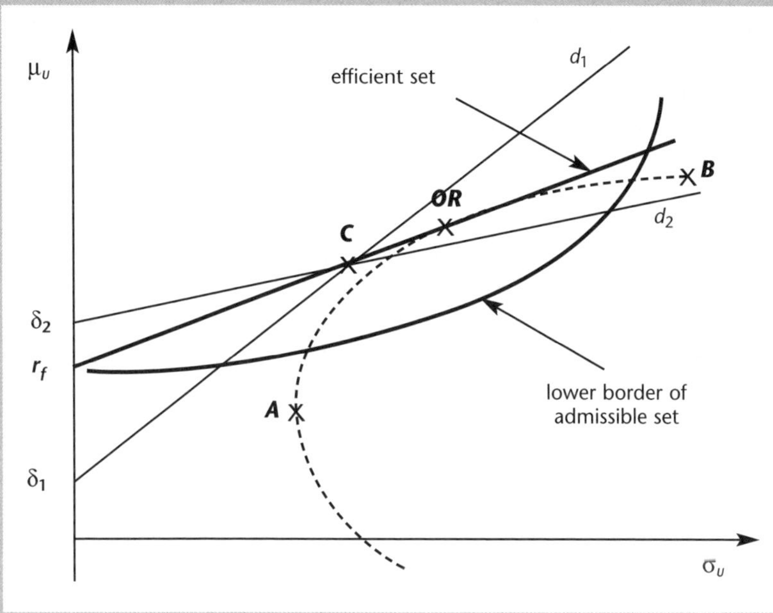

Figure 4.3 Portfolio choice with the CP rule under possible forced premature termination

According to the decision rule recommended, the choice will be made among those assets and portfolios that are part of both the admissible and the efficient set. Any variation in $u(w^*)$ or α within a given decision situation and thus under a given common distribution will shift the admissible set and its lower border such that different sections of the efficient set meet the necessary condition. The most preferred portfolio will again be determined by $P(u(R_T) = u(r_T) < \delta_1)$ and $P(u(R_T) = u(r_T) > \delta_2)$ in the manner discussed in section 4.2. They are indicated in Figure 4.3 by the two rays emanating from $(0, \delta_1)$ and $(0, \delta_2)$. The decision rule will again lead to a choice of diversified portfolios in all but very special cases. In Figure 4.3, the choice made is again labelled as portfolio *C*.

Again, further assumptions will have to be made to determine the exact form and location of the admissible set. Independent and normally distributed R_t could be one such assumption. To render the R_t identically distributed, rebalancing the portfolio's wealth after each period is required to restate the assets' initial weights. If it is also assumed that no withdrawals are made during the investment horizon, then the value of any asset or portfolio follows a martingale, a sub-martingale, or a super-martingale process, depending on the expected value of its R_t. Assets and portfolios with $E[R_t] = E[R] \geq 0$, will have $E[W_{t+1} \mid w_t] = (1+E[R]) \cdot w_t \geq w_t$, which defines a sub-martingale.[17] Assets and portfolios with $E[R_t] < 0$, will have the conditional expected value of their wealth follow a super-martingale process.

More precise statements about location and form of the admissible set would be possible by making more such assumptions, in combination with more assumptions on the utility index $u(.)$. But analyses of special cases are not the purpose of this treatise. Situations of decision under Knightian risk are characterised by the individual feeling able to assign probabilities to all possible outcomes of his or her actions. An analysis of how these probabilities are deduced in special cases is of no interest here.

4.4 DECISION RULES ADEQUATE FOR INFINITELY OFTEN REPEATED INVESTMENTS

The time dimension inherent in any investment renders it difficult to apply the concept of infinity to portfolio choice situations. Situations of infinitely often repeated investments require either an infinite investment horizon, or investment periods of no positive length. Investment periods of no positive length are incompatible with the time dimension inherent in any investment. Infinite investment horizons question the need to make a decision at all. If specific situations cannot be conceptualised within a chosen framework, no decision rule needs to be recommended for them.

Nevertheless, situations of infinitely many repeats can be regarded as the implicit background of most decision rules discussed in Chapter 3. Their implicit reliance on the law of large numbers simply postulates this. If so, such situations warrant a treatment simply because of their prominence. In addition, their discussion provides for revisiting the St Petersburg game and its influence on decision theory.

In addition, and apart from giving credit where credit is due, the treatment of situations of infinitely many repeats serves two further purposes. First, it illuminates the fact that probabilities are at the heart of any decision rule recommended for situations of Knightian risk, even when the law of large numbers can be applied. Second, the treatment again illustrates the necessity to achieve congruence between the decision situation, the decision rule recommended for it, and any justification for this recommendation.

To apply the law of large numbers, a decision situation must prevail that does not only consist of infinitely many repeats, but in which the investor is also concerned solely about the average of all results. Only in such a situation can the law of large numbers assert that the average result will in probability converge to the expected value of the gamble. This assertion must not be misinterpreted. The law of large numbers does not assert that the expected value will be obtained with certainty. The law of large numbers only asserts that the expected value will be obtained with probability one. This does not make the expected value a certain event. A clear distinction must be made between an event carrying probability one and a certain event. That the expected value carries probability one does not imply that other results are impossible. They just carry probability zero. It must thus be concluded that the law of large numbers, or any other theorem comprising an analogous statement,[18] does not turn a decision under risk into a decision under certainty.

To recommend that decisions be made according to the expected value thus translates into a recommendation that decisions be made in view of what event carries the highest probability. Since in the case of infinitely many repeats the average of all results will with probability one be equal to the expected value, it is natural to recommend decision rules comprising only the expected value. Such a recommendation can indeed be expected to gain widespread approval. But it must nevertheless be characterised as a probability-based decision rule. This is true for the general case of decisions under Knightian risk, and it is thus also true for any special application, like situations of portfolio choice.

The recommendation must change markedly if it is assumed that the gambler is concerned about more than the average result. This is especially the case if the threat of forced premature termination is introduced again. This has been a main feature in the discussion on finitely many repeats in section 4.3, and may, of course, be a main feature in the discussion on infinitely many repeats. Krelle, when discussing repeated gambles, also points out that a recommendation consisting of an expected value alone can only be made if incurred losses do not mean ruin'.[19] 'Ruin' may here be translated into 'forced premature termination'. It is evident that the prospect of 'ruin' in a decision situation of repeated gambles has not gone unnoticed. But it has received only moderate attention.

In fact, the prospect of ruin has also been considered with respect to the St Petersburg game. Fries (1842) devotes some thirteen pages to the problem of applying the expected value to the St Petersburg paradox and other games. The essence of his critique is that the expected value is meaningless if the prospect of likely losses is only met by the prospect of immense but very improbable gains.[20]

This is indeed the case with the St Petersburg game. For Bernoulli's 'fair entrance fee' of 20 units, the probability is 31/32 that the gambler will suffer a loss in any one trial. For an entrance fee of 10, the probability of suffering a loss is 15/16, and for an entrance fee of 5 this probability is still 7/8. The gambler's prospect of losing all of his or her initial wealth during the course of repeated trials is clearly apparent.

Here lies, hidden beneath the prominence of Bernoulli's 'moral expectation', another possible solution to the St Petersburg paradox. The expected value is a poor estimate of the perceived 'fair' value of a gamble, if the chances of winning any substantial amount are threatened by a chance of losing all initial wealth and being unable to play the game long enough to make the expected gain.

Shafer (1988) claims that this line of reasoning was once popular in the mid-19th century.[21] But it retreated in the face of the solutions that were based on expected values. In his treatise on the St Petersburg game, Menger (1934) devotes only one of 27 pages to probability-based solutions. Samuelson (1977) mentions bankruptcy in his survey of the contributions to the St Petersburg game only with regard to the feasibility of collecting infinite stakes,[22] and immediately returns to expected utility. This may serve as an indication of how much Bernoulli's solution dominated all others.

If for the St Petersburg game the probability of the gambler's ruin was easily computable, it might have achieved a higher standing as a possible solution to the paradox. It consequently might have achieved a higher standing within decision theory in general. But calculating the exact ruin probability was clearly beyond the means of 18th-century mathematics. Consequently, the expected value found its way into almost any decision rule, either normative or descriptive, in almost any decision situation, characterised by either single or repeated gambles. The implicit background of this preference index, infinitely often repeated games of chance, retreated.

Given the above line of reasoning, the recommendation for portfolio choice situations of infinitely many repeats is straightforward. If the average result and the utility it renders are the investor's only concern, then he or she may choose and may be recommended to choose according to the $E[U]$ associated with the portfolios. This decision rule corresponds to a choosing the MFE as the measure of false prediction. Expected values of transformed random variables may also be used, if the average result of this transformed random variable and the utility it renders are the only concern of the investor. One example would be a decision rule that corresponds to the MSFE as the measure of false prediction.

If the investor is also concerned about forced premature termination, then one possibility is to weigh the probability of termination against the promised gain. A possible decision rule in this situation would thus be

$$\Psi(G) = \psi\left(E[u(R)], P\left(\{W_{G,1} < w^*\} \cup \ldots \cup \{W_{G,\tau-1} < w^* \mid w_1, w_2, \ldots w_{t-2} > w^*\}\right)\right)$$

for a situation in which premature termination is forced by the portfolio's wealth W_t falling below w^* in any period t. Recommending decision rules for other kinds of forced premature termination or for voluntary termination is straightforward, and need not be discussed here in further detail.

Notes

1 Bawa (1978), p. 255.
2 See Feller (1968), pp. 248–51.
3 As has already been mentioned in section 3.2, it is the average of all gains and losses that is balanced, not the sum.
4 Krelle (1968), p. 174.
5 The detailed discussion in section 3.6 may thus seem redundant, since all of the decision rules are made to submit to the EU principle. It was nevertheless included because of their prominence within portfolio choice theory. That many of them fail to meet their objective also seemed worth demonstrating.
6 Samuelson (1977), p. 26.
7 There are other definitions. Merton (1975) distinguishes between the 'decision horizon' and the 'planning horizon'. The decision horizon refers to the period after which a decision has to be made again. The planning horizon refers to the period of time specified in the investor's utility function. Merton's 'decision horizon' thus coincides with our 'investment horizon'.
8 There do exist investments to the returns of which investors may well assign probability one. The return on money may be assigned probability one. The return on short-term government bills may be assigned probability one. Also, the return on government zero coupon bonds maturing at the end of the investment horizon seem apt to be assigned probability one. All these investments may be perceived to carry negligible default risk. There is also no reinvestment risk within the investment horizon. On the other hand, all investments are burdened with inflation risk. Under the Knightian risk setting, inflation is part of the state of nature and is thus included in all results.
9 Goldberger (1991), p. 30.
10 Holthausen (1981), p. 183.
11 Nevertheless, the author is unaware of any such recommendation.

12 To deny exact knowledge of the distribution, while at the same time assuming exact knowledge of the distributions' moments, seems prone to be inconsistent in any case. There seems to be no compelling reason why the decision-making individual should be capable of assigning 'known' moments to an unknown distribution.

13 For a brief discussion of multi-period decisions within EU theory see Alexander and Francis (1986), pp. 214–17. According to Bellman (1957) and Mossin (1968), maximising expected utility of terminal wealth can be achieved by selecting single-period efficient portfolios, if returns are independently and normally distributed in each investment period, and if the investor has positive but diminishing marginal utility of wealth and an isoelastic 'utility' function.

14 It dates back to J. Bernoulli (1713). See also Feller (1968), pp. 342ff. and 363ff.

15 The most comprehensive treatise of general situations consisting of repeated gambles is probably still Dubbins and Savage (1965).

16 Of course, if w^* is greater than r_f, the starting point does not correspond to any actual asset or portfolio. It is simply convenient to construct the lower border of the admissible set as if every point in ($\mu_{U,T}$, $\sigma_{U,T}$) space did correspond to an asset or portfolio.

17 According to Feller (1971), credit for developing the theory of martingales has to be given to J.L. Doob (1953). Applications of martingales to asset prices and portfolio values are found in, for example, Osborne (1959) and Samuelson (1965, 1973). A discussion of martingales in financial market theory is given by LeRoy (1989).

18 For example, the central limit theorem comprises such an analogous statement.

19 Krelle (1968), p. 172. He does not consider infinitely many repeats. He is concerned with calculating the number of plays needed to be able to rely on the expected value alone, for which he introduces thresholds of perceptibility.

20 Fries (1842), p. 116.

21 Both Shafer (1988) and Menger (1934) mention some sources.

22 This idea is expressed by Fry (1928), pp. 194–9.

CHAPTER 5

Conclusions

As the preceding analyses show, any recommendation on how to select a portfolio must first be based on a thorough analysis of the decision situation at hand. This analysis must include three aspects: the general theoretical framework that is to be applied, the characteristics of the decision situation, and a statement on which results of the action should matter to the decision-making individual.

The general framework chosen here is the field of decisions under Knightian risk. Within this framework, the characteristics of the decision situation are expressed by defining the set of actions, the set of states of nature, the set of results and the set of evaluated results. It has become evident that defining the set of results depends on the definition of the investment period and the investment horizon, that is, on whether the investment is repeated or not. That the definition of the set of results also depends on which results the individual should consider important is evident in any case. When the decision situation is analysed, and when Debreu's and Kolmogorov's axioms are accepted, recommendations can be made in the form of decision rules, which are then by definition normative in character.

The analysis of the decision situation at hand may also be used to evaluate whether a decision rule fits the situation it has been recommended for. The case is made that decision rules comprising some expected value are adequate only for very special situations. The case rests on the following arguments. The usual justification for many decision rules, and for the EU principle in particular, is to declare them 'rational'. This justification is vacuous. 'Rationality' is an empty phrase and may be assigned to any decision rule, no matter what it comprises.

Thus, further support for decision rules consisting of or including expected values has often been sought in some version of the law of large numbers. The law of large numbers has been the expected value's historic justification, and has remained an implicit support for all decision rules based on it. But the law of large numbers is only applicable under two conditions. First, the decision situation must incorporate infinitely many repeats. Second, the decision-making individual must solely be concerned about the average of all results.

If other events are of importance, decision rules consisting of expected values alone are inadequate. This result highlights the need to analyse the decision situation thoroughly before any recommendation can be made. In cases of single or finitely often repeated gambles, no version of the law of large numbers offers any support for expected values. If support is sought for such situations, it must be sought elsewhere.

To arrive at alternative recommendations, decision situations are analysed here from a different perspective. This different perspective is provided by the problem of prediction, which is closely related to decision problems. An analysis of the problem of prediction reveals that decision rules are nothing but recommendations to minimise a specific cost function, with 'costs' being some measure of predictive power. The newly defined criterion of 'adequacy' postulates that a decision rule and its underlying measure of predictive power fit the portfolio choice situation at hand. 'Adequate' decision rules are designed and recommended, and their functionality is demonstrated graphically. One important result of the graphical demonstrations is that such designed 'adequate' decision rules do recommend diversification behaviour in all situations. Recommending diversification has been declared a prerequisite for plausibility and acceptability of any decision rule to be applied to portfolio choice problems.

Although the graphical examples may lure one into thinking that nothing revolutionary has been offered, it is a fact that the new criterion of 'adequacy' demands the viewing of portfolio choice situations in a fundamentally different way. Having recourse to the problem of prediction, 'adequacy' introduces cost functions that in almost all decision situations are completely different from those commonly used in portfolio choice theory today. Decision rules used today implicitly rely on cost functions that are expected values, like MSE or MSFE. The criterion of adequacy says that single or infinitely often repeated gambles require cost functions employing other quantities than expected values. With the change in recommended cost functions comes the change in recommended decision rules, since cost functions and decision rules are interwoven. This has been shown for Markowitz's μ–σ^2 rule. Another example is the cost function $P(U) = 0$, where $U = X - c$ is the forecast error. In the discrete case, this cost function is obviously minimised by the mode. So the entire analysis of a decision situation rests on the chosen cost function, which translates into a decision rule.

When the cost function changes, and with it the decision rule, the entire analysis changes. 'Efficiency' receives a new meaning and portfolios that are part of the efficient set in (μ, σ^2) space may or may not be part of the efficient set in the new framework, regardless of whether the new efficient set is, with the help of Chebychev's inequality, actually drawn in (μ, σ^2) space. Previously optimal portfolios may not be optimal portfolios any more. Well-known and widely used measures of optimality, like the Sharpe ratio, become meaningless. A whole new set of definitions is required.

Changing the cost function also requires another look at the usefulness of performance measurement. Performance measurement is undertaken with the fact borne in mind that real life decision situations are not characterised by complete knowledge of all probabilities. Characteristics of any portfolio can thus only be claimed; they are never certain, nor can they be proven. It is only fair to feel a need to have the acclaimed characteristics tested. Unfortunately, this task is by no means easy. Testing a hypothesis with any statistical significance requires a certain number of observations of the random variable at hand, that is, of the gamble played, or the portfolio chosen. The number of observations required depends on the quantity to be tested and the distribution of an appropriate test statistic. It is again evident that a thorough analysis of the decision situation at hand is needed before any claims can be made on whether the number of observations necessary can in fact be obtained.

As has been shown, decision rules that employ expected values and that seek support in the law of large numbers implicitly assume decision situations that consist of infinitely many repeats. This implicit background may cause undue optimism. It may lead to thinking that observing a sufficient number of realisations for testing the hypothesised magnitude of the expected value was possible, at least in principle.[1]

But the analysis of Chapter 4 has shown that almost all decision situations of relevance are in fact decision situations in which the chosen gamble is only played once. One should not be enthusiastic about the amount of information that a single realisation of a random variable provides. Throwing a die once will reveal nothing on whether it is fair or loaded, and if so, what its expected value is. One realisation will also reveal nothing as to which value of the die has what probability. Decision situations that are properly described as situations in which the chosen gamble will be played only once will never provide enough information to decide whether the assumptions have been correct, and thus whether the choice made has been a good one. This fact is independent of, but accentuated by, the recommendation of probability-based decision rules. It should not keep one from applying the proper framework to portfolio choice problems.

Of course, in this treatise, not all aspects of decision making in portfolio choice situations are or can be covered. The many-faceted nature of portfolio selection problems simply forbids this. The concessions made will briefly be listed to acknowledge the fact that further considerations may be made.

First, the treatise focuses on normative decision rules. This allows the exclusion of almost any references to observed decision-making behaviour. The main reason is that descriptive decision theory is at odds with decision rules. The empirical falsification of Debreu's axioms forbids, strictly speaking, the use of decision rules within descriptive decision theory. Still, real-life aspects are not treated as totally irrelevant. The need to recommend diversification behaviour is stressed. Diversification of investments is declared recommendable per se, and diversification can also be observed. In addition, the decision rules recommended here bear some relevance with respect to empirical findings on decision making. For example, Halter and Dean (1971) cite some evidence that a threshold for unfavourable results exists for many individuals. Fishburn (1977) concludes that most individuals do exhibit a target return in investment contexts. Hershey and Shoemaker (1985) claim that there exists an 'aspiration level' phenomenon. Swalm (1966) reports to have detected target levels of return in corporate decision making. Green (1963) arrives at the same conclusion. The already cited empirical findings by Kahneman and Tversky (1979) and Allais (1953) also support the concept of target levels of return. Thus, the decision rules recommended here are not completely irrelevant from a real-life point of view, as some introspection may also confirm.

Second, the treatise is fairly general in nature. Its aim is to discuss basic axioms and fundamental assumptions in a general framework of portfolio choice. This general view stresses the necessity of complying with Debreu's and Kolmogorov's axioms, of clearly distinguishing between a normative and a positive stance, and of matching supportive reasoning for one or the other decision rule with the decision situation at hand. This general view stands in contrast to the very specific recommendations common in the literature today, which often disregard the above-mentioned necessities. For the purpose of achieving general consistency, no detailed decision rules need to be designed. It suffices to specify the decision rules up to which information to include. Accordingly, the decision situation and the individuals' possible preferences are never described in every detail.

For the sake of presentational ease and to achieve comparability with decision rules recommended elsewhere, the graphical demonstration of decision rules relies on Chebyshev's inequality. The demonstration is thus conveniently given within the familiar (μ, σ) space. The general nature is also helpful in illuminating the influence that the St Petersburg paradox has had up to the present day. The general nature of the discussion allows a discussion to be included on the history of thought on decision situations, and on the differences between situations of games of chance and situations of portfolio choice.

The drawback of such a general discussion is that there is no room for every possible extension. No single asset types are specified, and not every possible decision situation is characterised. Still, many possible extensions can be discussed within the general framework without much difficulty. The generality of the treatise does not keep its results from being applicable to specific situations and extensions.

For example, variable or relative levels of favourable and unfavourable results may also be modelled. The recommended decision rules may then be applied by defining favourable and unfavourable results appropriately. The simultaneous consideration of assets and liabilities can be modelled by defining the random variable R as the difference between the value of assets and liabilities at any point in time. Thus, the entire field of 'asset–liability management' may be treated within the framework introduced here.

The task would not be simple.[2] Constant change in assets and liabilities due to cash flows and valuation changes requires either a convenient definition of investment period and investment horizon, or a dynamic modelling approach in which an encompassing gamble is designed from a multitude of single gambles. But the recommendation according to the criterion of adequacy would apply. No matter how probabilities are arrived at, if the decision situation is one in which the same gamble is played only once or finitely often, the recommended decision rule should be based on these probabilities. Dynamic optimisation of any expected value, a frequent approach within asset–liability management, would only be adequate if the decision situation could be repeated infinitely often.

The third and undoubtedly biggest concession made in this treatise is embedding the analysis within the framework of decisions under Knightian risk. The assumption that the decision-making individual feels able to attach 'degrees of belief' to every possible result of his or her action is clearly heroic. But it is a convenient assumption when addressing problems that are at the core of any decision situation. No attention is diverted towards problems of estimation and inference. Thus, similar assumptions are made in other works on decision making in portfolio choice situations, notably also by Markowitz.

The fact that probabilities are not known in real-life decision situations causes two problems. First, ways and means have to be found to arrive at some sort of estimate of the probabilities needed. At first sight, this seems impossible, given the sheer number of estimates needed and the limited amount of information and observations available. But some shortcuts could be employed to arrive at practical solutions. One such shortcut would be to model returns and their utilities according to a 'factor model'. This is the same approach that Sharpe (1963) suggested for reducing the number of estimates needed for applying Markowitz's model.

To make the CP rule applicable in practice in this manner, first, a common distribution of all explanatory variables, that is, the 'factors', needs to be assumed or estimated. Second, the factors' influence on the explained variables, that is, on the assets' returns or their utilities, needs to be modelled. Third, the distribution of the residuals needs to be estimated, and some assumption on their mutual interrelations and their interrelations with the factors is needed.

With this set of information, Monte Carlo simulations can be run to estimate the probabilities specified in the decision rule for single assets and their combinations. Thus, the optimal combination of assets can be simulated and choices according to the CP rule can be made. Obviously, the task is still formidable, and the number of simulations needed calls for superior computing resources.

The second problem posed by the fact that probabilities are not known in real-life decision situations is that any recommendation must incorporate the inherent uncertainties in the estimates. Thus, statistical decision rules need to be recommended, which account for the need to collect information on the distributions of the results, and consider the inferences that have to be made from the information gathered. The problems of estimation and inference in decision theory have not gone unnoticed, and it might be argued that Markowitz is wrong in stating that this was 'another story'.[3] In 1986, Alexander and Francis stated: 'It took roughly 20 years for at least the first part of this story to be told. The complete story is one that promises to keep researchers busy for some time.'[4]

Nothing in this treatise contributes to that story. The standpoint taken is intentionally different, not because problems of estimation, inference and applicability are considered inconvenient or inferior. It is taken because it allows a focused analysis of the core problem of decision making in situations in which the result of a decision made is not known in advance. For a focused analysis, additional problems of estimation are better set aside. Thus the stage is cleared and the similarity of choice and prediction can be illuminated, the close connection between cost functions and decision rules can be explained, and the case can be made that decision rules should be 'adequate' for the decision situation they are recommended for.

Notes

1 The actual problems are still insurmountable; see, for example, Ippolito (1993).
2 For the difficulties encountered in asset–liability management, and some sophisticated solutions, see Nager (1998).
3 Markowitz (1959), p. 91.
4 Alexander and Francis (1986), p. 93.

References

Albach, H. (1962) Zur Finanzierung von Kapitalgesellschaften durch ihre Gesellschafter, *Zeitschrift für die gesamte Staatswissenschaft*, vol. 118, pp. 65–87.

Alexander, G.J. and Francis, J.C. (1986) *Portfolio Analysis*, 3rd edn, Englewood Cliffs, NJ, Prentice-Hall.

Allais, M. (1953) Le comportement de l'homme rationnel devant le risque: Critique des postulats et axiomes de l'école américaine, *Econometrica*, vol. 21, pp. 503–46.

Allais, M. (1986) Determination of a cardinal utility according to an intrinsic invariant model, in Daboni, L., Montesano, A. and Lines, M. (eds) *Recent Developments in the Foundations of Utility and Risk Theory*, Dordrecht, Reidel.

Allais, M. (1987) The general theory of random choices in relation to the invariant cardinal utility function and the specific probability function, the (U, θ) model: a general overview, in Munier, B.R. (ed.) *Risk, Decision and Uncertainty*, Dordrecht, Reidel.

Arrow, K.J. (1971) *Essays in the Theory of Risk Bearing*, Chicago, Markham.

Balzer, L.A. (1994) Measuring investment risk: a review, *Journal of Investing*, vol. 3, pp. 47–58.

Baumol, W.J. (1968) An expected gain–confidence limit criterion for portfolio selection, *Management Science*, vol. 10, pp. 174–82.

Bawa, V.S. (1975) Optimal rules for ordering uncertain prospects, *Journal of Financial Economics*, vol. 2, pp. 95–121.

Bawa, V.S. (1976) Safety first, stochastic dominance, and optimal portfolio choice, Bell Laboratories Economic Discussion Paper no. 60.

Bawa, V.S. (1978) Safety first, stochastic dominance, and optimal portfolio choice, *Journal of Financial and Quantitative Analysis*, vol. 13, pp. 255–71.

Bawa, V.S. and Lindenberg E.B. (1977) Capital market equilibrium in a mean–lower partial moment framework, *Journal of Financial Economics*, vol. 5, pp. 189–200.

Beard, R.E., Pentikäinen, T. and Personen E. (1969) *Risk Theory*, London, Methuen.

Bell, D. (1982), Disappointment in decision making under uncertainty, *Operations Research*, vol. 30, pp. 961–81.

Bellman, R. (1957) *Dynamic Programming*, Princeton, Princeton University Press.

Bernoulli, D. (1738) Specimen Theoria Novae de Mensura Sortis, Commentarii Academiae Scientiarum Imperialis Petropolitanae, Tomus V, pp. 175–92. A version translated by Sommer, L. is given as 'Exposition of a new theory of risk', *Econometrica*, vol. 22, 1954, pp. 23–6.

Bernoulli, J. (1713) Ars Conjectandi, opus posthumum. Accedit Tractatus de Seriebus Infinitis, et Epistola Gallice Scriptae de Lupo Pilae Recticularis, Basel, Impensis Thurnisiorum, Fratrum.

Black, F. (1972) Capital market equilibrium with restricted borrowing, *Journal of Business*, vol. 45, pp. 444–55.

Blattberg, R.C. and Gonedes, N.J. (1974) A comparison of the stable and student distributions as statistical models for stock prices, *Journal of Business*, vol. 47, pp. 244–80.

Blume, M.E. and Friend, I. (1975) The asset structure of individual portfolios and some implications for utility functions, *Journal of Finance*, vol. 30, pp. 585–603.

Brennan, M.J. (1971) Capital market equilibrium with divergent borrowing and lending rates, *Journal of Financial and Quantitative Analysis*, vol. 6, pp. 1197–205.

Buschena, D.E. (1992) The effects of alternative similarity on choice under risk: toward a plausible explanation of independence violations of the expected utility model, unpublished PhD dissertation, University of California at Berkeley, Department for Agricultural and Resource Economics.

Buschena, D.E. and Zilberman, D. (1994a) The effects of alternative similarity on risky choice: implications for violations of expected utility, working paper, Montana State University, Bozeman, Department for Agricultural Economics and Econometrics.

Buschena, D.E. and Zilberman, D. (1994b) What do we know about decision making under risk and where do we go from here?, *Journal of Agricultural and Resource Economics*, vol. 19, pp. 425–45.

Cramér, H. (1930) On the mathematical theory of risk, *Försäkringsaktiebolaget Skandias Festskrift*, Stockholm, Centraltryckeriet, pp. 7–84.

Debreu, G. (1954) Representation of a preference ordering by a numerical function, in Thrall, R.M., Coombs, C.H. and Davis, R.L. (eds) *Decision Processes*, New York, John Wiley & Sons, pp. 159–65.

Debreu, G. (1959) *The Theory of Value*, New York, John Wiley & Sons.

De Finetti, B. (1937) La prévision: Ses lois logiques, ses sources subjectives, *Annales Institut Poincaré*, vol. 7, pp. 1–68.

DeGroot, M.H. (1982) Decision theory, in Kotz, S. and Johnson, N.L. (eds) *Encyclopedia of Statistical Sciences*, vol. 2, New York, John Wiley & Sons.

Domar, E.V. and Musgrave, R.A. (1944) Proportional income taxation and risk-taking, *Quarterly Journal of Economics*, vol. 40, pp. 389–422.

Doob, J.L. (1953) *Stochastic Processes*, New York, John Wiley & Sons.

Dubbins, L.E. and Savage, L.J. (1965) *How to Gamble If You Must*, New York, McGraw-Hill.

Dyl, E.A. (1975) Negative betas: the attractions of selling short, *Journal of Portfolio Management*, vol. 1, pp. 74–6.

Fama, E.F. (1965a) The behavior of stock market prices, *Journal of Business*, vol. 38, pp. 34–105.

Fama, E.F. (1965b) Portfolio analysis in a stable paretian market, *Management Science*, vol.11, pp. 404–19.

Fama, E.F. (1976) *Foundations of Finance*, New York, Basic Books.

Fama, E.F. and Miller, M.H. (1972) *The Theory of Finance*, Hinsdale, Ill., Holt, Rinehart & Winston.

Feller, W.F. (1945) Note on the law of large numbers and 'fair' games, *Annals of Mathematical Statistics*, vol. 16, pp. 301–4.

Feller, W.F. (1971) *An Introduction to Probability Theory and its Applications*, vol. I, 3rd edn, New York, John Wiley & Sons.

Feller, W.F. (1968) *An Introduction to Probability Theory and its Applications*, vol. II, 2nd edn, New York, John Wiley & Sons.

Fishburn, P.C. (1964) *Decision and Value Theory*, New York, John Wiley & Sons.

Fishburn, P.C. (1977) Mean-risk analysis with risk associated with below-target returns, *American Economic Review*, vol. 67, pp. 116–26.

Fishburn, P.C. (1982) Non-transitive measurable utility, *Journal of Mathematical Psychology*, vol. 26, pp. 31–67.

Freund, R.J. (1956) The introduction of risk into a programming model, *Econometrica*, vol. 24, pp. 253–64.

Friedman, M. and Savage, L.J. (1948) The utility analysis of choices involving risk, *The Journal of Political Economy*, vol. 56, pp. 279–304.

Friend, I. and Blume, M.E. (1975) The demand for risky assets, *American Economic Review*, vol. 65, pp. 900–22.

Fries, J.F. (1842) Versuch einer Kritik der Principien der Wahrscheinlichkeitsrechnung, Braunschweig, Verlag Friedr. Bieweg und Sohn, reprinted in König, G. and Geldsetzer, L., *Jakob Friederich Fries, Sämtliche Schriften*, vol. 14, pp. 11–254, Aalen, Scientia Verlag, 1974.

Fry, T.C. (1928) *Probability and its Engineering Uses*, New York, Van Nostrand.

Gnedenko, B.V. and Kolmogorov, A.N. (1954) *Limit Distributions for Sums of Independent Random Variables* (trans. by K.L. Chung), Reading, Mass., Addison-Wesley.

Goldberger, A.S. (1991) *A Course in Econometrics*, Cambridge, Mass., Harvard University Press.

Graham, B. and Dodd, D. (1934) *Security Analysis*, New York, McGraw-Hill.

Green, P.E. (1963) Risk attitudes and chemical investment decisions, *Chemical Engineering Progress*, vol. 59, pp. 35–40.

Grether, D.M. and Plott, C.R. (1979) Economic theory of choice and the preference reversal phenomenon, *American Economic Review*, vol. 69, pp. 623–38.

Hadar, J. and Russel, W.R. (1969) Rules for ordering uncertain prospects, *American Economic Review*, vol. 59, pp. 25–34.

Hadar, J. and Russel, W.R. (1971) Stochastic dominance and diversification, *Journal of Economic Theory*, vol. 3, pp. 288–305.

Hagen, O. (1979) Towards a positive theory of preferences under risk, in Allais, M. and Hagen, O. (eds) *Expected Utility Preference and the Allais Paradox: Contemporary Discussions of Decisions under Uncertainty with Allais' Rejoinder*, Dordrecht, Reidel.

Hagerman, R.L. (1978) More evidence on the distribution of security returns, *Journal of Finance*, vol. 33, pp. 1213–221.

Halter, A.N. and Dean, G.W. (1971) *Decisions under Uncertainty*, Cincinnati, South-Western Publication Company.

Hanoch, G. and Levy, H. (1969) The efficiency analysis of choices involving risk, *Review of Economic Studies*, vol. 36, pp. 335–46.

Harlow, W.V. (1991) Asset allocation in a downside-risk framework, *Financial Analysts Journal*, vol. 47, pp. 28–40.

Harlow, W.V. and Rao, R.K.S. (1989) Asset pricing in a generalized mean–lower partial moment framework: theory and evidence, *Journal of Financial and Quantitative Analysis*, vol. 23, pp. 285–311.

Hershey, J.C. and Shoemaker, P.J.H. (1985) Probability versus certainty equivalence methods in utility measurement: are they equivalent?, *Management Science*, vol. 31, pp. 1213–31.

Hicks, J.R. (1939) *Value and Capital*, Oxford, Clarendon Press.

Hogan, W.W. and Warren, J.M. (1972) Computation of the efficient boundary in the E-S portfolio selection model, *Journal of Financial and Quantitative Analysis*, vol. 7, pp. 1881–96.

Hogan, W.W. and Warren, J.M. (1974) Toward the development of an equilibrium capital-market model based on semivariance, *Journal of Financial and Quantitative Analysis*, vol. 9, pp. 1–11.

Holthausen, D.M. (1981) A risk–return model with risk and return measured as deviations from a target return, *American Economic Review*, vol. 71, pp. 182–8.

Hoskins, C.G. (1973) Distinctions between risk and uncertainty, *Journal of Business Finance*, vol. 5, pp. 10–12.

Hsu, D.-A., Miller, R. and Wichern, D. (1974) On the stable paretian behavior of stock-market prices, *Journal of the American Statistical Association*, vol. 69, pp. 108–13.

Ippolito, R.A. (1993) On studies of mutual fund performance, *Financial Analysts Journal*, vol. 23, pp. 1962–91.

Kahneman, D. and Tversky, A. (1979) Prospect theory: an analysis of decision under risk, *Econometrica*, vol. 47, pp. 263–91.

Karmarkar, U. (1974) The effect of probabilities on the subjective evaluation of lotteries, working paper no. 698–74, Massachusetts Institute of Technology, Sloane School of Management.

Kataoka, S. (1963) A stochastic programming model, *Econometrica*, vol. 31, pp. 181–96.

Khintchine, A. (1929) *Comptes rendus de l'Académie des Sciences*, Paris, vol. 189, pp. 477–9.

Knight, F.H. (1921) *Risk, Uncertainty and Profit*, New York, Houghton Mifflin.

Kolmogorov, A. (1933) *Grundbegriffe der Wahrscheinlichkeitsrechnung*, Berlin, Springer-Verlag.

Kon, S.J. (1984) Models of stock returns – a comparison, *Journal of Finance*, vol. 39, pp. 147–65.

Krelle, W. (1968) *Präferenz- und Entscheidungstheorie*, Tübingen, J.C.B. Mohr (Paul Siebeck).

Kroll, Y., Levy, H. and Markowitz, H.M. (1984) Mean-variance versus direct utility maximization, *Journal of Finance*, vol. 49, pp. 47–61.

Lange, O. (1944) *Price Flexibility and Employment*, Bloomington, Ind., Principia Press.

Leland, J.W. (1990) A theory of approximate expected utility maximization, working paper, Carnegie-Mellon University Pittsburgh, Department for Social and Decision Sciences.

LeRoy, S.F. (1989) Efficient capital markets and martingales, *Journal of Economic Literature*, vol. 27, pp. 1583–621.

Levy, H. and Markowitz, H.M. (1979) Approximating expected utility by a function of mean and variance, *American Economic Review*, vol. 69, pp. 308–17.

Lévy, P. (1924) *Calcul des Probabilités*, Paris, Gauthier-Villars.

Lévy, P. (1937) *Théorie de l'Addition des Variables Aléatoires*, Paris, Gauthier-Villars.

Libby, R. and Fishburn, P.C. (1977) Behavioral models of risk taking in business decision: a survey and evaluation, *Journal of Accounting Research*, vol. 15, pp. 272–92.

Loomes, G. and Sudgen, R. (1982) Regret theory: an alternative theory of rational choice under uncertainty, *Economic Journal*, vol. 92, pp. 805–24.

Luce, R.D. and Raiffa, H. (1957) *Games and Decisions*, New York, John Wiley & Sons.

McCord, M. and de Neufville, R. (1983) Empirical demonstration that expected utility decision analysis is not operational, in Stigum, B.P. and Wenstop, F. (eds) *Foundations of Utility and Risk Theory with Applications*, Dordrecht, Reidel.

Machina, M.J. (1982) 'Expected utility' analysis without the independence axiom, *Econometrica*, vol. 50, pp. 227–323.

Mandelbrot, B. (1963) The variation of certain speculative prices, *Journal of Business*, vol. 36, pp. 394–419.

Mao, J.C.T. (1970a) Survey of capital budgeting: theory and practice, *Journal of Finance*, vol. 25, pp. 349–60.

Mao, J.C.T. (1970b) Models of capital budgeting, E-V vs. E-S, *Journal of Financial and Quantitative Analysis*, vol. 4, pp. 657–75.

Markowitz, H.M. (1952) Portfolio selection, *Journal of Finance*, vol. 7, pp. 77–91.

Markowitz, H.M. (1959) *Portfolio Selection: Efficient Diversification of Investments*, New York, John Wiley & Sons.

Markowitz, H.M. (1991) *Portfolio Selection: Efficient Diversification of Investments*, 2nd edn, New York, John Wiley & Sons.

Marschak, J. (1938) Money and the theory of assets, *Econometrica*, vol. 6, pp. 311–25.

Massé, M.P. and Morlat, M.G. (1953) Sur le classement économique des perspectives aléatoires, in Centre National de la Recherche Scientifique (ed.) *Econométrie* (Colloque intern. d'Econométrie du 12 au 17 mai 1952), pp. 165–99.

May, K.O. (1954) Intransitivity, utility, and the aggregation of preference patterns, *Econometrica*, vol. 22, pp. 1–13.

Menger, K. (1934) Das Unsicherheitsmoment in der Wertlehre. Betrachtungen im Anschluss an das sogenannte Petersburger Spiel, *Zeitschrift für Nationalökonomie*, vol. 51, pp. 459–85.

Merton, R.C. (1972) An analytic derivation of the efficient portfolio frontier, *Journal of Financial and Quantitative Analysis*, vol. 7, pp. 1851–72.

Merton, R.C. (1975) Theory of finance from the perspective of continuous time, *Journal of Financial and Quantitative Analysis*, vol. 10, pp. 659–74.

Mossin, J. (1968) Optimal multiperiod portfolio policies, *Journal of Business*, vol. 41, pp. 215–29.

Munier, B.R. (1988) A guide to decision making under uncertainty, in Munier, B.R. (ed.) *Risk, Decision and Uncertainty*, Dordrecht, Reidel.

Nager, J. (1998) Innovative Ansätze im Asset-liability-management, in Kleeberg, J.M. and Rehkugler, H. (eds) *Handbuch Portfoliomanagement*, Bad Soden/Ts., Uhlenbruch.

Officer, R. (1972) The distribution of stock returns, *Journal of the American Statistical Association*, vol. 67, pp. 807–12.

Osborne, M.F.M. (1959) Brownian motion in the stock market, *Operations Research*, vol. 7, pp. 145–73.

Porter, R.B. (1974) Semivariance and stochastic dominance: a comparison, *American Economic Review*, vol. 64, pp. 200–4.

Pratt, J.W. (1964) Risk aversion in the small and in the large, *Econometrica*, vol. 32, pp. 122–36.

Pruitt, D.G. (1962) Pattern and level of risk in gambling decisions, *Psychological Review*, vol. 69, pp. 187–201.

Quirk, J.P. and Saposnik, R. (1962) Admissibility and measurable utility functions, *Review of Economic Studies*, vol. 29, pp. 140–6.

Ramsey, F.P. (1931) *The Foundation of Mathematics and other Logical Essays*, London, Routledge & Kegan Paul.

Reichling, P. (1996) Safety First-Ansätze in der Portfolio Selektion, *Zeitschrift für betriebswirtschaftliche Forschung*, vol. 48, pp. 31–48.

Richter, M.K. (1959/60) Cardinal utility, portfolio selection and taxation, *Review of Economic Studies*, vol. 27, pp. 152–66.

Ross, S.A. (1982) On the general validity of the mean-variance approach in large markets, in Sharpe, W.F. and Cootner, C.M. (eds), *Financial Economics: Essays in Honor of Paul Cootner*, Englewood Cliffs, NJ, Prentice-Hall.

Roy, A.D. (1952) Safety first and the holding of assets, *Econometrica*, vol. 20, pp. 431–49.

Rubinstein, A. (1988) Similarity and decision making under risk: is there a utility theory resolution to the Allais paradox?, *Journal of Economic Theory*, vol. 46, pp. 145–53.

Samuelson, P.A. (1952) Probability, utility, and the independence axiom, *Econometrica*, vol. 20, pp. 670–8.

Samuelson, P.A. (1965) Proof that properly anticipated prices fluctuate randomly, *Industrial Management Review*, vol. 6, pp. 41–9.

Samuelson, P.A. (1973) Proof that properly discounted present values of assets vibrate randomly, *Bell Journal of Economics and Management Science*, vol. 4, pp. 369–74.

Samuelson, P.A. (1977) St. Petersburg paradoxes: defanged, dissected, and historically described, *Journal of Economic Literature*, vol. 15, pp. 24–55.

Savage, L.J. (1954) *The Foundations of Statistics*, New York, John Wiley & Sons.

Schneeweiß, H. (1963) Nutzenaxiomatik und Theorie des Messens, *Statistische Hefte*, vol. 4, p. 178.

Schneeweiß, H. (1967) *Entscheidungskriterien bei Risiko*, Berlin, Springer-Verlag.

Shafer, G. (1988) The St. Petersburg paradox, in Kotz, S. and Johnson, N.L. (eds) *Encyclopedia of Statistical Sciences*, vol. 8, pp. 865–70.

Sharpe, W.F. (1963) A simplified model of portfolio analysis, *Management Science*, vol. 9, pp. 277–93.

Sheynin, O.B. (1972) D. Bernoulli's work on probability, *RETE Strukturgeschichte der Naturwissenschaften*, vol. 1, pp. 273–300.

Shoemaker, P.J.H (1982) The expected utility model: its variants, purposes, evidence and limitations, *Journal of Economic Literature*, vol. 20, pp. 529–63.

Stegmüller, W. (1973) *Probleme und Resultate der Wissenschaftstheorie und Analytischen Philosophie*, vol. IV, 1. Halbband, Personelle Wahrscheinlichkeit und Rationale Entscheidung, Berlin, Springer-Verlag.

Stone, B.K. (1973) A general class of three-parameter risk measures, *Journal of Finance*, vol. 28, pp. 675–85.

Sugden, R. (1986) New developments in the theory of choice under uncertainty, *Bulletin of Economic Research*, vol. 38, pp. 1–24.

Swalm, R.D. (1966) Utility theory – insights into risk taking, *Harvard Business Review*, vol. 47, pp. 123–36.

Telser, L.G. (1955/56) Safety first and hedging, *Review of Economic Studies*, vol. 23, pp. 1–16.

Thomas, H.A. Jr. (1958) A method of accounting for benefit and costs uncertainties in water resource project design, mimeo, Harvard Program in Water Resources.

Tobin, J. (1958) Liquidity preference as behavior towards risk, *Review of Economic Studies*, vol. 36, pp. 65–86.

Tobin, J. (1965) The theory of portfolio selection, in Hahn, F.H. and Brechling, F.P.R. (eds) *The Theory of Interest Rates*, London, Macmillan (now Palgrave).

Von Neumann, J. and Morgenstern, O. (1944) *Theory of Games and Economic Behaviour*, Princeton, Princeton University Press.

Wald, A. (1950) *Statistical Decision Functions*, New York, John Wiley & Sons.

Whitmore, G.A. (1970) Third order stochastic dominance, *American Economic Review*, vol. 50, pp. 457–9.

Yaari, M.E. (1987) The dual theory of choice under risk, *Econometrica*, vol. 55, pp. 95–115.

INDEX